Getting Ahead

Communication Skills for Business English

Learner's Book

*Sarah Jones-Macziola
& Greg White*

CAMBRIDGE
UNIVERSITY PRESS

Published by the Press Syndicate of the University of Cambridge
The Pitt Building, Trumpington Street, Cambridge CB2 1RP
40 West 20th Street, New York, NY 10011-4211, USA
10 Stamford Road, Oakleigh, Victoria 3166, Australia

© Cambridge University Press 1993

First published 1993

Printed in Great Britain by Redwood Press, Melksham

ISBN 0 521 407079   Learner's Book
ISBN 0 521 407044   Learner's Book Cassette
ISBN 0 521 407060   Home Study Book
ISBN 0 521 407052   Home Study Book Cassette
ISBN 0 521 407036   Teacher's Guide
ISBN 0 521 448697   Home Study Book CD

Acknowledgements

The authors would like to thank their colleagues at Insearch Language Centre, University of Technology, Sydney, Australia, and at International House, Freiburg, Germany, especially Dieter Löffner, and also Sue Unwin-Späth and Peter Späth of Freiburg, Germany.

The authors and publishers would like to thank the following institutions and teachers for their help in piloting and commenting on the material and for the invaluable feedback which they provided.

Renate Stocker, Internationales Sprachzentrum an der Universität Graz, Austria. Rogério da Costa Neves, Peter J. Patterson and Vania Stewart, Britannia Executive School, Rio de Janeiro, Brazil. Marco Tyler-Williams, New Start Comunicaçoes, Rio de Janeiro, Brazil. Anita Subtil and Robin A. Forrest, Group Ecole Supérieure de Commerce et d'Industrie de l'Ain, Bourg-en-Bresse, France. David Podger, ESC, Le Havre, France. Isobel Drury and Tessa Pacey, ILC, Paris, France. Peggy-Anne Pye, VHS Nürnberg, Germany. Christine Frank, Wedermark-Bissendorf, Germany. Pam Scott, The British Council, Athens, Greece. Rachel Borland and Claire O'Connor, Josiah's Institute of English & Commerce, Hong Kong. Nick Noakes, The British Council, Hong Kong. Susan Garvin, The British Institute, Florence, Italy. S. Magee, British School Company Services, Rome, Italy. Francesco Recchini, ITC Sandro Botticelli, Rome, Italy. Vincent Broderick, Soai College, Osaka, Japan. Eden Brough, Glen Giffen, Andrew Grimes, Chris Musial, Ruth Singleton and Richard Smith, ILC, Tokyo, Japan. Lisa Hori, Tokyo Foreign Language Centre, Tokyo, Japan. Tess Kennedy and Colin de Búria, INTERPERKS, Barcelona, Spain. Bryan Robinson, Granada, Spain. Sue Tomlinson, International House Executive Centre, Madrid, Spain. Lesley Gruit, Dil Danismanlik Hizmetleri, Istanbul, Turkey. Alex Teasdale and Nilbahar Ekinci, The Istanbul Turco British Association, Istanbul, Turkey. Christine Mannheim, London, UK.

The authors and publishers are grateful to the following copyright owners for permission to reproduce copyright material. Every endeavour has been made to contact copyright owners and apologies are expressed for any omissions.
p. 12: logos reproduced by permission of AEG (UK) Ltd, AT&T (UK) Ltd, BASF plc, BMW (GB) Ltd, IBM United Kingdom Ltd, ICI is a registered trademark of Imperial Chemical Industries PLC, JVC (UK) Ltd. p. 16: logos reproduced by permission of The Boeing Company, The Broken Hill Proprietary Company Ltd, 'Coca-Cola' is a registered trademark of The Coca-Cola Company, Lufthansa German Airlines, Sony Consumer Products UK, Volvo Car UK Ltd.

pp. 38(©1991), 79(©1990), 94(©1990), 98(©1989), 102(©1990): text reprinted with permission from WORKING WOMAN magazine. Copyright by W.W.T. Partnership. p. 38: information in illustration by permission of Ricoh UK Ltd. p. 66: advertisement adapted from an advertisement for 1989 by permission of the China External Trade Development Council. p. 79: cartoon reprinted from New Yorker. p. 85: by permission of Filofax Group plc. p. 97: from This Month in Bath. p. 101: by permission of Soundview Executive Book Summaries (5 Main St, Bristol, VT 05443, USA, phone 802-453-4062, fax 802-453-5062). p. 117 (file 17): from The Independent on Sunday by permission of The Independent. p. 121 (file 16): from The Independent on Sunday by permission of The Independent.

The authors and publishers are grateful to the following illustrators and photographic sources:

Illustrators: Angela Barnes: pp. 66, 68, 69. Julia Bishop-Bailey: pp. 16, 48. Colin Bunner: pp. 86-87. Peter Byatt: pp. 75, 96, 110. Paul Chappell: pp. 10, 26, 98. Paul Collicut: p. 78. David Downton: pp. 43, 88, 93. Richard Eckford: pp. 44, 89. Clive Goodyer: p. 18. Edward McLachlan: pp. 9, 53, 91. Michael Ogden: pp. 42, 82. Giovanna Pearce: pp. 30-31. Martin Salisbury: pp. 7, 36. Sunita Singh: pp. 58-59. Sue Smickler: pp. 114-115. George Taylor: pp. 15, 21, 22, 23, 33, 38, 55, 63, 76, 100, 105, 106, 108. John York: pp. 4, 5, 8.

Cover illustration by Giovanna Pearce.

Photographers / Photographic sources: Apple Computer UK Ltd: p. 19 tr. The J. Allan Cash Photolibrary: p. 94 tr. Coca-Cola Great Britain and Ireland: p. 19 c. 'Coca-Cola' is a registered trademark of The Coca-Cola Company. Colorific Photo Library Ltd: p. 54 bl. Greg Evans International: p. 57. Chris Fairclough Colour Library: pp. 25 r, 37 r, 60. Susan Griggs Agency: pp. 54 tl, 66, 94 bl. Robert Harding Picture Library: pp. 25 c, 52 r, 54 bc, br. The Image Bank: pp. 25 l, 37 c, 65 tr, br, 94 br. Nigel Luckhurst: pp. 12, 50, 62, 83. Mercedes-Benz (United Kingdom) Ltd: p. 17. Miele Company Ltd: p. 29. Picturepoint-London: p. 6 bc. Renault (UK) Ltd: p. 19 l. Bill Robinson: p. 34. 'A Shell Photograph': p. 19 br. Sony Consumer Products Company UK: p. 113. Spectrum Colour Library: pp. 6 tl, 37 l, 61, 64 r, 65 l. Tony Stone Photo Library: pp. 6 tc, tr, ml, mc, mr, bl, br, 11, 52 l, 80, 95, 97. The Telegraph Colour Library : p. 64 l. 'ZEFA' Picture Library: pp. 54 tr, 92, 94 tl, c.

l = left   c = centre   r = right   t = top   m = middle
b = bottom

Picture Research by Sandie Huskinson-Rolfe (PHOTOSEEKERS).

Contents

Unit 1 Introductions and greetings 4
  1.1 Introducing yourself
  1.2 Saying where you're from
  1.3 Introducing other people

Unit 2 Occupations 10
  2.1 Saying what you do
  2.2 Telephoning
  2.3 Finding out information about people

Unit 3 Companies 16
  3.1 Describing a company
  3.2 Talking about types of business
  3.3 Finding the perfect partner

Unit 4 The place of work 22
  4.1 Giving directions
  4.2 Talking about departments
  4.3 Taking a message

Unit 5 Revision and consolidation 28

Unit 6 Day-to-day work 32
  6.1 Talking about your work
  6.2 Describing routines
  6.3 Likes and dislikes

Unit 7 The working environment 38
  7.1 Asking people to do things
  7.2 Talking about stress
  7.3 Giving advice

Unit 8 Plans 44
  8.1 Discussing arrangements
  8.2 Making appointments
  8.3 Planning a trip

Unit 9 Visits and travel 50
  9.1 Talking to a visitor
  9.2 Attending business events
  9.3 Reserving a hotel room

Unit 10 Revision and consolidation 56

Unit 11 Work history 60
  11.1 Finding someone a job
  11.2 Talking about your career
  11.3 Describing your first job

Unit 12 Fairs and sales 66
  12.1 Finding out about a trade fair
  12.2 Talking about products
  12.3 Placing an order

Unit 13 Product description 72
  13.1 Comparing products
  13.2 Saying what's best
  13.3 Making suggestions

Unit 14 Entertaining 78
  14.1 Taking a guest to dinner
  14.2 Making invitations
  14.3 Describing food

Unit 15 Revision and consolidation 84

Unit 16 Firms and factories 88
  16.1 Visiting a factory
  16.2 Saying what you've done
  16.3 The company report

Unit 17 The Business Pleasure Trip 94
  17.1 Finding out about a city
  17.2 Making offers
  17.3 Thanking

Unit 18 Problems, problems 100
  18.1 Dealing with problems
  18.2 Complaining and apologizing
  18.3 Finding a solution

Unit 19 Future trends 106
  19.1 Making predictions
  19.2 Talking about the future
  19.3 Changing the way we work

Unit 20 Revision and consolidation 112

Files 116

Tapescripts 123

Wordlist with phonetic transcription 131

UNIT

1 Introductions and greetings

1.1 Introducing yourself

A What do you do when you meet someone for the first time?

What do people do in different countries?

B 🖭 Listen to these introductions.

Now introduce yourself to someone else.

C 🔲 Mr Robinson comes to your company. You don't know him.
Listen to these conversations.

D Study these examples.

I'm Mario Bendetti.		my
Are you Carol Anglin?	Yes, I am.	your
Is your name Napton?	No, it isn't.	its

Complete these three conversations. Then practise them.

A: Excuse me, is .... name Marriot?

B: No, it .... name's Crossman.

A: Oh, I'm sorry, Ms Crossman.

C: Excuse me, ... Mike Watson?

D: Yes, ...

C: .... Roger Miller. Pleased to meet you.

E: ...., are you Mr Nawab?

F: No, ... I'm Mohamed Farique.

E: Oh, ..., Mr Farique.

1.2 Saying where you're from

A Look at the advertisement. Do you know where these cities are?

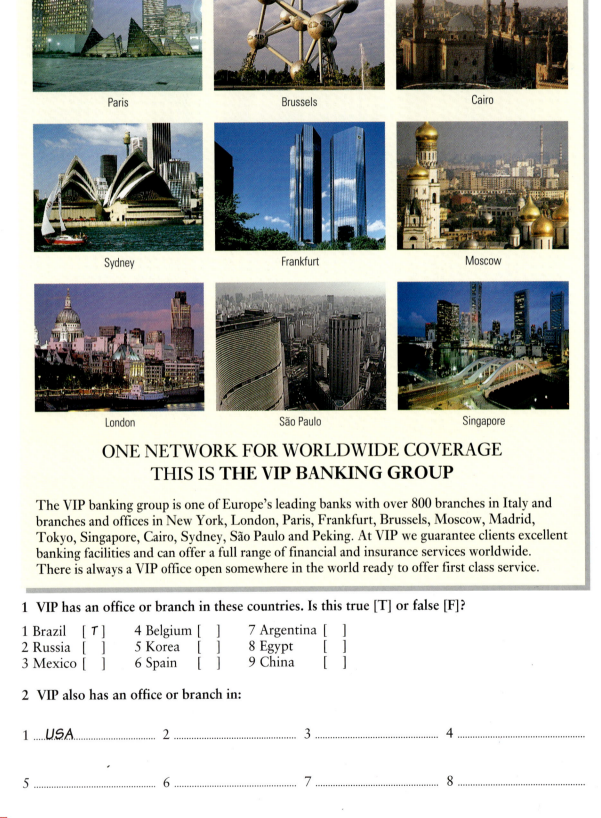

Paris

Brussels

Cairo

Sydney

Frankfurt

Moscow

London

São Paulo

Singapore

ONE NETWORK FOR WORLDWIDE COVERAGE
THIS IS **THE VIP BANKING GROUP**

The VIP banking group is one of Europe's leading banks with over 800 branches in Italy and branches and offices in New York, London, Paris, Frankfurt, Brussels, Moscow, Madrid, Tokyo, Singapore, Cairo, Sydney, São Paulo and Peking. At VIP we guarantee clients excellent banking facilities and can offer a full range of financial and insurance services worldwide. There is always a VIP office open somewhere in the world ready to offer first class service.

1 VIP has an office or branch in these countries. Is this true [T] or false [F]?

1 Brazil [T]	4 Belgium [ ]	7 Argentina [ ]
2 Russia [ ]	5 Korea [ ]	8 Egypt [ ]
3 Mexico [ ]	6 Spain [ ]	9 China [ ]

2 VIP also has an office or branch in:

1 ....USA................   2 ....   3 ....   4 ....

5 ....   6 ....   7 ....   8 ....

B   VIP has a conference each year. Listen to the five short conversations and match the name to the branch.

NAME		BRANCH
1 Anopow	[ ]	Brussels
2 Braun	[ ]	Frankfurt
3 Brown	[ ]	Peking
4 Santos	[ ]	Paris
5 Girardin	[ ]	São Paulo
6 Le Grand	[1]	Moscow
7 Pousset	[ ]	Paris
8 Yin	[ ]	New York

Listen again. What do the people say?

GREETING

RESPONSE

1 How are you?   ....

2 ....   Pleased to meet you.

3 How do you do?   ....

4 Nice to see you again.   ....

5 ....   Hi.

C   Listen and mark the stress.

1 <u>How</u> do you do?

2 Nice to see you again.

3 Pleased to meet you.

4 Hello, how are you?

Practise saying these sentences.

1.3 Introducing other people

A Read the dialogue and then listen to the recording. Is it the same?

Alice: Hello, Giovanni. Good to see you again. How are you?
Giovanni: Just fine, fine. And you?
Alice: Oh, not too bad. Giovanni, do you know Bryan Turner?
           Bryan, this is Giovanni Toncini. He's from Italy. He works in Rome.
Bryan: Pleased to meet you, Mr Toncini.
Giovanni: Please, call me Giovanni.
Bryan: And I'm Bryan.
Alice: Have a seat, Giovanni.
Giovanni: Thank you.
Alice: How about some coffee? Giovanni?
Giovanni: Yes, please. Black with sugar, please.

B Introduce your partner to someone else.

C Match the phrases with a suitable response.

1 Bye.
2 Have a nice weekend.
3 Nice to talk to you.
4 Goodbye and thank you for your help.

A That's all right. Goodbye.
B Thank you. You too.
C See you on Friday.
D It was nice talking to you, too.

Monday
Tuesday
Wednesday
Thursday
Friday
Saturday
Sunday

Listen and check your answers. Then practise the conversations with a partner.

2 Occupations

2.1 Saying what you do

A 🔊 Listen. Is it Robert Brown or George Braun?

abc Software
Robert Brown
Sales Manager

155 Sansome Street
San Francisco, CA 94101, USA
Tel: 415 / 433 - 1743 Fax: 415 / 433 - 0432

abc Software
George Braun
Software Engineer

155 Sansome Street
San Francisco, CA 94101, USA
Tel: 415 / 433 - 1743 Fax: 415 / 433 - 0432

B Match the pictures to the job.

1

2

3

4

5

6

A I'm an accountant. D I work in the export department.
B I'm a secretary. E I'm an engineer.
C I'm a sales clerk. F I'm the Marketing Manager.

Is your profession or job here? If not, what is your profession or job in English?
Find out about the others like this:

What do you do?

　I'm a(n) …

　I work in …

C 🔲 Listen and mark the stress.

1 acc<u>ou</u>ntant
2 export
3 secretary
4 engineer
5 marketing

D Look at the jobs in the box. Which people are:

professional and technical workers?
administrative workers?
clerical and office workers?

accountant	secretary	lawyer
typist	engineer	sales manager
receptionist	executive	supervisor

🔲 Listen to someone talking about the workforce in Singapore. Check your answers.

Listen again and fill in the percentages on the pie chart.

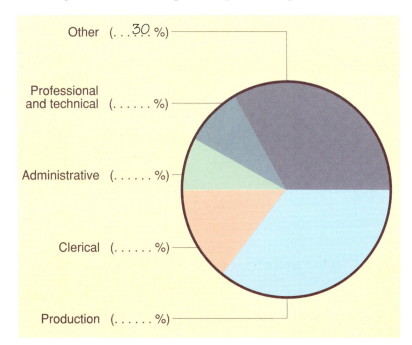

Other (....30.%)

Professional and technical (......%)

Administrative (......%)

Clerical (......%)

Production (......%)

2.2 Telephoning

A 🔲 Listen to Richard Lampl on the phone. How many people does he talk to? Who does he want to talk to?

B Say the names of these companies.

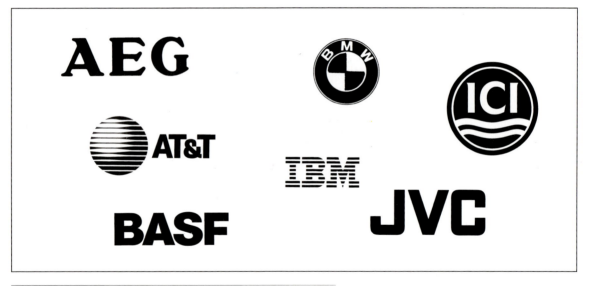

What other companies have names like this?

C Notice what you say when something is not clear.

Can you spell that, please?
How do you spell that?

Can you repeat that, please?
Can you say that again, please?

Practise spelling people's names. Student A looks at File 1 on page 117
and Student B looks at File 2 on page 121.

D Practise this dialogue with a partner.

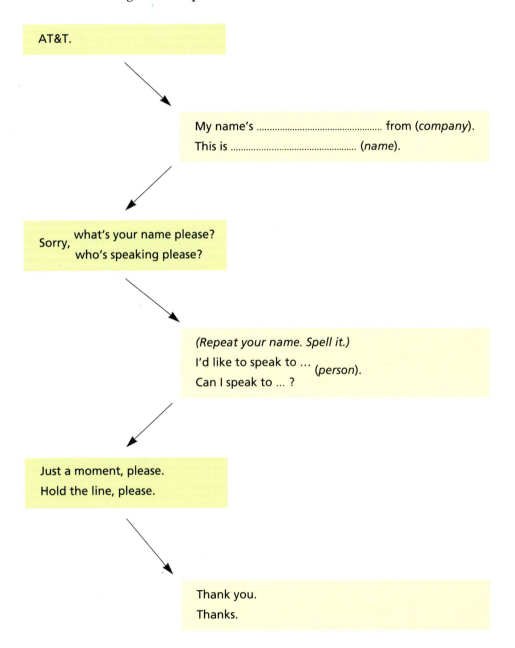

AT&T.

My name's .... from (*company*).
This is .... (*name*).

Sorry, what's your name please?
who's speaking please?

(*Repeat your name. Spell it.*)
I'd like to speak to ... (*person*).
Can I speak to ... ?

Just a moment, please.
Hold the line, please.

Thank you.
Thanks.

2.3 Finding out information about people

A In many countries it is essential to have a business card. You give the card to your business partner and he or she can see the name of your company as well as address and telephone and telefax numbers. The card also lets your partner know your position in the company or your occupation.

B What information is missing on these business cards? What questions can you ask to find out the information?

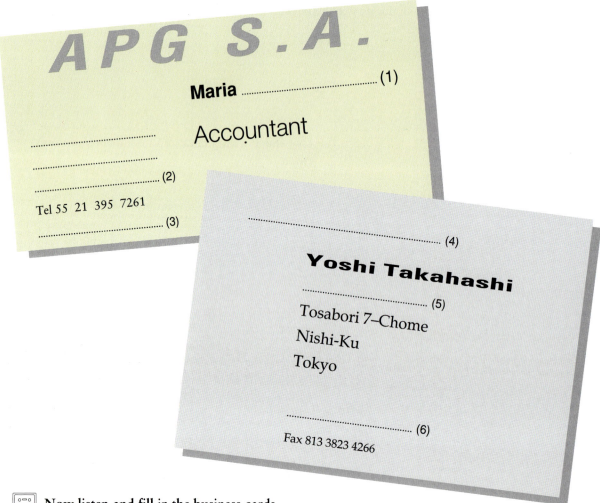

A P G S . A .

Maria .... (1)

Accountant

....
....
.... (2)

Tel 55 21 395 7261

.... (3)

.... (4)

Yoshi Takahashi

.... (5)

Tosabori 7–Chome

Nishi-Ku

Tokyo

.... (6)

Fax 813 3823 4266

Now listen and fill in the business cards.

Listen again. What questions do the people ask?

1 ....

2 ....

3 ....

4 ....

5 ....

6 ....

Now practise the conversations.

C Study these telephone numbers.

320 112	three two oh	double one two
	three two zero	one one two
3823 4266	three eight two three	four two double six

Listen to these telephone numbers and say them.

1	545 760	6	854 166
2	485 255	7	322 752
3	613 1002	8	553 0067
4	348 1991	9	757 3658
5	684 4521	10	605 7331

D Work in pairs. You need information about some people. Student A looks at File 3 on page 122 and Student B looks at File 4 on page 118.

'. . . that's it, Thomas. I'm now officially on holiday.'

3 Companies

3.1 Describing a company

A Read the company description and look at the map. Which company is it?

We have 63,600 employees worldwide and sales of $13,716m. We manufacture cars, trucks, buses, marine and industrial engines. We also work in the aerospace industry. Our position as a major international group with large operations in Europe and North America is a result of quality, safety and caring for people and the environment.

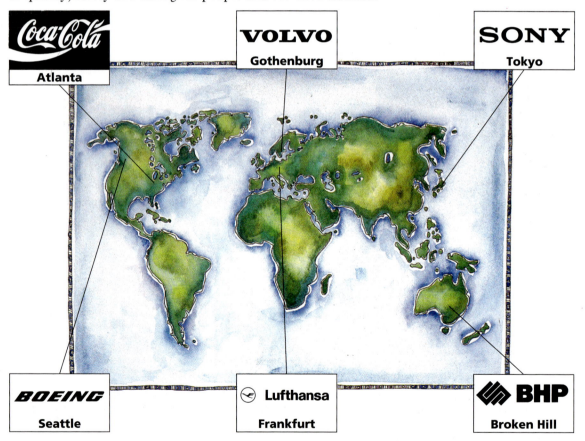

Talk about the companies like this:

Coca-Cola is an American company.
The headquarters are in Atlanta.
It has/hasn't got branches in my country.

B Look at these companies. Do you know where their headquarters are?

Daimler-Benz   Brother   Fiat   Levi Strauss
Siemens   Toyota   Gucci   Microsoft

Munich	Osaka	Turin	New York
Stuttgart	Nagoya	Florence	San Francisco
Erlangen	Tokyo	Milan	Seattle

Compare with your partner like this:

Coca-Cola is an American company.

I think the headquarters are in San Francisco.
No, they're not. They're in Atlanta.

I think the headquarters are in Atlanta.
That's right. They are.

C 🔲 Listen to three people talking about their companies. Complete the profiles.

1 Company: *Goldstar Electric* ....

Nationality: ....

Headquarters: ....

No. of branches: ....

2 Company: ....

Nationality: ....

Headquarters: ....

Offices: *Worldwide* ....

3 Company: ....

Nationality: ....

Headquarters: ....

No. of plants: ....

D Find out about your partner's company and make notes. You can ask questions like these:

Who do you work for?
Is that an (American) company?
Where are the headquarters?
Do you have branches in (Europe)?

Now tell the others about your partner's company.

Pierre works for (company).
They're a (British) company.
Their headquarters are in (city).
They have branches in (countries).

3.2 Talking about types of business

A Match the type of business to the pictures.

> electronics   motor vehicles   financial services
> chemicals   telecommunications   aerospace
> energy   engineering   travel & tourism

1 ....

2 ....

3 ....

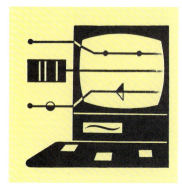

4 ....

5 ....

6 ....

7 ....

8 ....

9 ....

Can you think of more types of business?

B   Make some sentences about these companies.

Coca-Cola		cars and trucks.
Gucci		soft drinks.
Rank Xerox	makes	chemicals.
Ciba-Geigy	produces	clothing.
Apple	manufactures	oil.
Renault	sells	office equipment.
Heinz		food.
Shell		computers.

C   Some companies don't make things. They offer services.
Match the company to the service.

1 Dentsu is in the	[ ] airline business.
2 Lloyds of London is in the	[ ] travel and tourism business.
3 ITT/Sheraton is in the	[ ] insurance business.
4 McDonalds is in the	[ ] banking business.
5 Club Med is in the	[1] advertising business.
6 Lufthansa is in the	[ ] hotel business.
7 Crédit Lyonnais is in the	[ ] restaurant business.

D   Study these examples.

What does Ford produce?	Does Ford produce cars?
It produces cars.	Yes, it does.
What do Toyota and Nissan make?	Do Toyota and Nissan make computers?
They make cars.	No, they don't.

Complete the questions with *do* or *does*.

1 .... PepsiCo make clothing?
2 What .... Ford and General Motors do?
3 What .... Kodak sell?
4 .... Microsoft make computers?
5 .... Matsushita and Sony manufacture consumer electronics?
6 What .... your company produce?

What are the answers to the questions?

Work with a partner. Now think of six more questions about companies. Ask another pair.

3.3 Finding the perfect partner

A Read the advertisement for Sunkyong and find out what these figures refer to.

1 $9 billion
2 2000
3 36
4 $800 million
5 10022

In the East, it's one of the best known companies

In the West, it's one of the best kept secrets

SUNKYONG

A perfect partner for your business

Sunkyong is one of Korea's leading business groups with annual sales of more than $9 billion. We produce a wide range of products, from oil, chemicals and plastics to fibres, textiles and magnetic media. And we sell over 2000 products in 36 countries. In the U.S. alone, we have sales of over $800 million.

If you are looking for a perfect partner, please contact:

Sunkyong U.S.A., Inc., Dept. F
110 East 55th Street
New York, NY 10022
Fax: (212) 906-8127

Read the advertisement again. Are these sentences true [T] or false [F]?

1 Sunkyong is an American company.   [   ]
2 It is in the energy business.   [   ]
3 It's also in the insurance business.   [   ]
4 It sells its products all over the world.   [   ]

B Work in pairs. Find out some information about two other companies.
Student A looks at File 5 on page 120 and Student B looks at File 6 on page 117.

C Complete this letter.

MicroComp Pty Ltd
231 Shoreway Road
Belmont, CA 94002.

TAINAN ELECTRICAL

10 Cheng Kung Road
Tainan
Taiwan
Tel: (06) 2289101
Fax: (06) 2268502

Dear Sir or Madam:

January 15, 199–

We are looking for a company who can help us distribute our products in new markets.

We manufacture 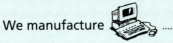 ....1) components. At present we export

to ....2), but we would like to export to ....3).

Enclosed please find our brochure which gives details of our company.

We look forward to hearing from you.

Sincerely,

D You work for a Mexican company: Intermex S.A.
Lucio Blanco No. 441
02400 Mexico, D.F.
Mexico

1 You produce

2 You export to

3 You want to export to

Write a similar letter to the:

Singatech
25 River Valley Road
Singapore 0924

Don't forget the reader's address, your address and the date.

4 The place of work

4.1 Giving directions

A 🔲 Listen to the receptionist talking to three visitors and fill in the missing departments in the directory.

Directory

4th Floor: **Research and Development**
Purchasing

3rd Floor: ....
Sales

2nd Floor: **Accounts**

....

1st Floor: ....
Canteen

Ground Floor: **Dispatch**
Production
Reception

B Read the note and mark Miss Ho's office on the plan.

Dear Mr. Souza
I'm sorry that I'm not in my office to meet you.
I'm in Miss Ho's office. Please take the elevator to
the 4th floor. Come out of the elevator, go right
then turn left. Miss Ho's office is the second
on the right, it's opposite the photocopying
room.
Mr. Chang

STORE ROOM

PHOTOCOPYING ROOM

CONFERENCE ROOM

ELEVATOR

Listen to the conversations, and mark these places on the plan.

1 Mr Lee's office
2 Ms Wong's office
3 Mr Tan's office

C Practise this dialogue with a partner.

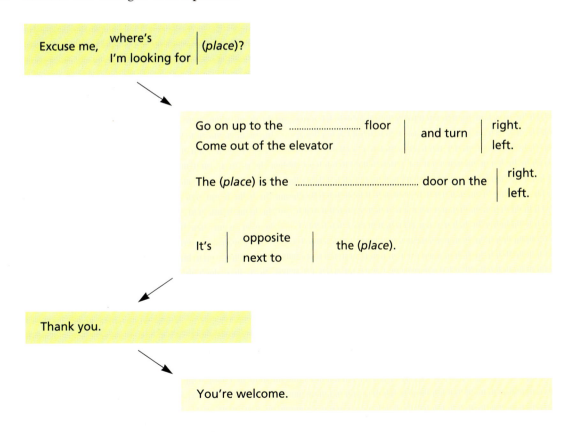

| Excuse me, | where's | (place)? |
| | I'm looking for | |

| Go on up to the .... floor | and turn | right. |
| Come out of the elevator | | left. |

| The (place) is the .... door on the | right. |
| | left. |

| It's | opposite | the (place). |
| | next to | |

Thank you.

You're welcome.

D Draw a plan of your company, training centre or school. Tell your partner how to find your room. Or use Files 7 and 8 on pages 120 and 119.

4.2 Talking about departments

A Match the department with its duties.

1 Marketing   [ ] develops new products.
2 Personnel   [ ] helps customers with problems.
3 Accounts   [1] advertises and markets products.
4 Research and Development   [ ] organizes payment.
5 Sales   [ ] sends goods to customers.
6 Dispatch   [ ] buys goods for the company.
7 Purchasing   [ ] sells the company's products.
8 Production   [ ] makes goods in the factory.
9 After-sales   [ ] deals with employees.

🖭 Listen and check your answers.

Is your department here? What does it do?

B 🖭 These words have two syllables. Listen and mark the stress.

1 <u>pro</u>duct   3 accounts   5 research
2 problem   4 payment   6 dispatch

These words have three syllables. Listen and mark the stress.

7 <u>mar</u>keting   10 customer   13 employee
8 develops   11 purchasing   14 organize
9 personnel   12 production   15 department

Now practise saying them.

C Read these letters and mark the department they should go to.

1 After-sales [ ]   2 Personnel [ ]
   Accounts   [ ]   Marketing [ ]
   Sales   [ ]   Dispatch [ ]

Cameronics
Boomjes 36,
3006 Rotterdam,
The Netherlands

Ms Mahoud
Lian Heng Enterprises
38 Napier Road
Singapore 1025

24 January 199-

Dear Ms Mahood

Thank you for the prompt delivery of our order
no. C00145. Please find enclosed a cheque for
US$ 3,600 in payment of your invoice no. 5731
of 15 January 199-.

Yours sincerely

L. van der Linde

L. van der Linde

Tel 31-10-474 1788
Fax 31-10-474 3517

Calle Canillas 7
E2 3H
28002 Madrid
Spain

Fasco Textiles
13 Grafton Street
London W1 31X
England

6 February 199-

Dear Sir or Madam

I refer to your advertisement in last month's
edition of "Textile World" for a sales
representative in Spain.

I enclose a c.v. which gives details of my experience
in the textile trade in Spain.

I look forward to hearing from you.

Yours faithfully

María Salgado

3 R & D   [ ]
   Purchasing [ ]
   Production [ ]

4 Sales   [ ]
   Marketing [ ]
   Accounts   [ ]

Office Systems Pty Ltd
124 Oak Street
Chatswood
NSW 2067
Australia

Mr Son Young
New Asia Inc
Miwon Building   Tel (61-2) 419 3209
43 Yomido-dong   Fax (61-2) 419 4011
Yongdungpo-ku
Seoul   1 February 199-

Dear Mr Son Young

Thank you for your enquiry of 28 January about our products.

We enclose our catalogue and price list with details of discounts and delivery dates.

If you require any further information, please contact me. We look forward to hearing from you.

Yours sincerely

Angelica Rosetti
Angelica Rosetti

BRACOM S.A.
Rua Martin Franscisco
01226 São Paulo
Brazil

Tel ##55 11/8266 1210
Fax ##55 11/8266 2951

Howard Inc
291 Caxton Street
Sante Fe
New Mexico 87501
USA

Dear Sir/Madam   7 February 199-

We are a publisher of business magazines and commercial trade journals and can offer special advertising rates to new customers.

This is an excellent chance for your company to increase the market for your products in South America.

Enclosed please find copies of two of our magazines. If you have any further questions, do not hesitate to contact us.

Truly yours

J. Pontas

J. Pontas

<u>Underline</u> the words in each letter which helped you decide on the correct department.

D 🔲 Listen to three people talking about their work. Which department do they work in?

1 Maria   [ ] Sales.
2 Carl   works in   [ ] Personnel.
3 Regina   [ ] Marketing.
                            [ ] Accounts.
                            [ ] After-sales.

4.3 Taking a message

A 📼 Listen to this telephone call. Is the information on the message correct?

PHONE MESSAGE

Message: _none_ ....

....

FOR: *Mr Suzuki*

....

DATE: *3.12*   TIME: *9.45*

FROM: *Ms Piondi*

....

OF: *Viva Agency*

PHONE: *39 - 2 - 67 78 90 12*

[x] Will call again

[ ] Please Call

[ ] Wants to see you

B Why aren't these people in the office? Match the picture to the reason.

A She's in the factory.
B They're in a meeting.
C He's with a customer.
D She's on holiday.
E They're at lunch.
F He's ill.

C Study these examples.

> **in** + the factory; Frankfurt; Japan
> **at** + lunch; a conference
> **on** + holiday; a business trip

Now complete these sentences with the correct preposition.

1 Anna's .... lunch.
2 Mr Harding's .... a conference.
3 Ms Harris is .... the warehouse.
4 Frank's .... vacation.
5 Peter's .... Head Office.
6 Ms Taylor .... Brazil.
7 Paul's .... a business trip.
8 Janet's .... Paris.

▭ Listen and check your answers.

D Practise this dialogue with a partner.

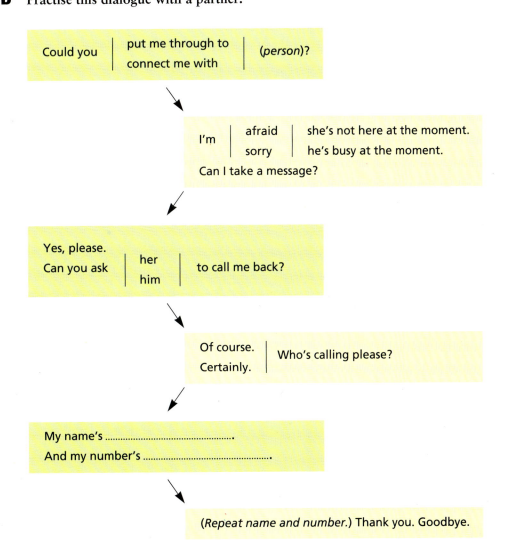

| Could you | put me through to / connect me with | (person)? |

I'm | afraid | she's not here at the moment.
      | sorry | he's busy at the moment.
Can I take a message?

Yes, please.
Can you ask | her / him | to call me back?

Of course. / Certainly. | Who's calling please?

My name's ....
And my number's ....

(Repeat name and number.) Thank you. Goodbye.

5 Revision and consolidation

A   What do you say? Match the function to the actual words.

1 Introduce yourself.	A We're in telecommunications.
2 Answer the phone.	We make and sell telephones.
3 Ask where something is.	B This is Gina Adams speaking.
4 Greet a colleague.	C What do you do?
5 Ask someone about their job.	D Hello. My name's Derek Scott.
6 Ask to speak to someone on the phone.	I work in Accounts.
7 Introduce a colleague.	E Excuse me. I'm looking for Mr Borge's office.
8 Say what your company does.	F This is Michelle Dupont.
	She's from our Paris office.
	G Hello, Andreas. How are you?
	H Can you put me through to Ms Turner?

Work in pairs. Write a short dialogue with some of the phrases.

B   Vocabulary Look at the words in the box and put them into groups.

production	chemicals	engineer	tourism	office assistant	accounts
personnel	receptionist	insurance	financial services	accountant	dispatch

JOBS	DEPARTMENTS	LINES OF BUSINESS
....	....	....
....	....	....
....	....	....
....	....	....

Add more words to each group.

....	....	....
....	....	....
....	....	....
....	....	....

C Reading Read the article and answer the questions.

FROM A STAFF OF FIVE TO A TURNOVER OF £18M

Miele, the German domestic appliance manufacturer, has been in the UK for thirty years.

The company started with a small office in central London, a staff of five and a turnover in the first 16 months of £53,000. Today it has a modern headquarters at Abingdon, near Oxford, employs about 200 people and has a turnover of £18 million.

The British company, like the other overseas subsidiaries, is a sales operation. Abingdon is an ideal town for the UK headquarters. It is very central as a distribution point and only five miles north of the 'inland port' of Milton.

The Miele group employs 13,500 people worldwide. But it is still a family concern. 'There is regular contact with headquarters in Gütersloh, Germany', says Herr Wedekind, chief executive of the British subsidiary.

The group sells its products to up-market customers in shops like Harrods and advertises in publications like *The Sunday Times* magazine. 'We sell our products to people who want quality, want the best, good after-sales service and trouble-free appliances', says Herr Wedekind.

1 Are these sentences true or false?

A Miele is a German company.
B The headquarters are in London.
C Miele employs 13,500 people in the UK.
D The company has an annual turnover of £53,000.
E The company manufactures in the UK.
F Herr Wedekind is the managing director in the UK.

Correct the sentences which are false.

2 Here are the answers to some questions. What are the questions?

A Abingdon.
B £18 million.
C 200.
D Washing machines, fridges, cookers.
E No, it doesn't. It only distributes domestic appliances.
F No, it isn't. It's a German company.

D Listening Listen to the interview with Geoff Story, the managing director of Donaldson Packaging. Make notes about the company.

E Speaking Play this game with a partner.

You are at a conference.

Play with a coin:

Heads – move one square.
Tails – move two squares.

Have conversations with your partner on each square.

START

1 You arrive at the conference. Introduce yourself to the receptionist.

2 The receptionist asks you to spell your name.

The receptionist asks you to spell your address.

20 Your colleague speaks very fast. What do you say?

21 Ask this man a question.

22 Give a colleague your business card.

A colleague asks you where your assistant is. Tell him/her.

19 A colleague wants to know what your company does. Tell him/her.

18 You make a phone call. Ask to speak to Mr Scotti.

17 A colleague asks you about the department you work in.

16 Move forward to 21.

A colleague wants some information about your company.

4
Move forward to 7.

5
You see a friend. Greet him/her.

6
Introduce your colleague to another person.

7
Ask this man a question.

8
You don't understand your colleague. What do you say?

Miss a turn.

24
Go back to 21.

25
It's time to go home. Say goodbye to your colleagues.

FINISH

9
A colleague asks you about your job. Tell him/her what you do.

10
A colleague asks you where your boss is. Tell him/her.

14
Ask this woman a question.

13
Go back to 9.

12
A colleague wants your phone number.

11
You want to make a phonecall. Ask where the phone is.

Day-to-day work

6.1 Talking about your work

A Read the two articles. Which work conditions are better?

1   en.   but influence overseas
           headquarters

el
ot
K's
to

Office hours are usually
from 9am to 6pm, although
many people work until 7 or
8pm. Junior staff normally
stay until their bosses leave.

nd
ull
lly

offices are usually open on
Saturday from 9am until
3pm. Lunch time begins at
1pm and lasts 1 hour.

of
be   Business meetings often
the   take a long time to organise

2   organisations like
    chambers of commerce.

T
an
of
A
co

Business hours usually start
at 9am and finish at 5pm,
Monday to Friday. Offices
are normally closed on
Saturdays. In many
businesses there is a 35 hour
working week. Lunch hour
begins at 12 and finishes at
1pm.

D
th
ev
m
in
re

Business meetings are
usually organised by

sp
go

B Study these examples.

at 9 o'clock, 5.30
on Monday, Friday afternoon
in May, August
from 12 to 1

Ask your partner questions like these.

What time do you start work?   *When do you finish work?*
When's the lunch break?   *Do you work on Saturdays?*
Do you have other breaks?   *When do you take your holiday?*

Make notes on what you find out.

C Look at these people. What hours do you think they work?

Compare your answers with a partner's.

D Two American colleagues are coming to work in your company. Write them a short letter describing the working conditions in your company.

Start like this:

```
Dear ...

Welcome to our company. Let me tell you
about our routine:

We start work at ...
```

Finish like this:

```
If you have any further questions,please
contact me.

Yours sincerely
```

6.2 Describing routines

A Read this article. Do you think Prue Leith works hard?

A Day in the Life of Prue Leith

Prue Leith, recently Businesswoman of the Year, was born in 1940. At 25 she started Leith's Good Food, a small catering company. Turnover is now £8 million, she employs 350 staff and on a good day is responsible for 15,000 meals.

Sometimes I get up at five, but when I can I sleep much later. I start the day with a cup of tea, but I rarely have breakfast. I just don't feel hungry in the morning. Some days I teach at our Cordon Bleu school, on others I sit behind my computer at home, but most of the time I'm in London, visiting kitchens and going to meetings.

I live in the Cotswolds, about an hour from the office in London. I normally take the train to London. I love travelling by train. It gives me time to relax and think.

I usually get to the office at about half past seven. During the day I speak to many people on the telephone and meet them as well.

I always have lunch in one of my restaurants – to see how the chefs are doing. I eat with colleagues, but we don't just talk about work.

On a normal day I work until about 7 pm. Then I go home to a TV dinner with my husband. He helps in the business, but we hardly ever discuss work in the evenings because we are too tired.

In an average week I have two or three business dinner appointments with clients, staff and managers.

I go to bed at eleven or twelve o'clock and so I get five or six hours sleep. I sometimes take a pile of papers with me, but I always finish off reading a book. I always sleep well because I never know what I am going to do tomorrow until I look in my diary.

B Study these examples.

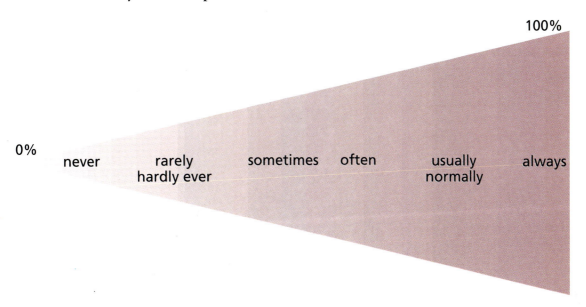

Use the words in the box to complete these sentences about Prue Leith.

1 She .... has breakfast.
2 She .... takes the train to work.
3 She .... gets to the office at 7.30.
4 She .... has lunch in a restaurant.
5 She .... discusses business with her husband.
6 She .... knows what she is going to do tomorrow.

Tell your partner about your day.

C Make some sentences about yourself.

I	meet customers go on trips entertain visitors write reports use English work late	once twice three times	a	day. week. month. year.

Now find out about a partner. You can ask questions like these:

Do you ever … ?
How often do you … ?

6.3   Likes and dislikes

A   Look at what people say about their jobs.

Which conditions are important for:

someone who wants to make a fortune?
someone with a family?
you?

Compare your answers with a partner's.

B Listen to three people talking about their jobs. Mark the things they talk about.

	1 Ros	2 Jan	3 Ute
boss			
colleagues			
hours			
holidays			
salary			
commuting			

Listen again. What things do they like? What things don't they like?

C Study these examples.

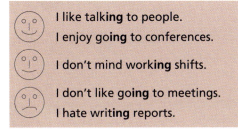

I like talk**ing** to people.
I enjoy go**ing** to conferences.

I don't mind work**ing** shifts.

I don't like go**ing** to meetings.
I hate writ**ing** reports.

Complete these sentences about yourself.

1 I .... talking to people.

2 I .... making phone calls.

3 I .... making phone calls in English.

4 I .... working with a computer.

5 I .... going to meetings.

6 I .... writing reports.

7 I .... working on my own.

8 I .... working on Saturdays.

Add more things you like and don't like doing. Then compare your list with a partner's. What is the same and what is different?

7 The working environment

7.1 Asking people to do things

A   Before you read the article mark the things a manager usually does.

opens the post [   ]   makes photocopies [   ]
does the filing [   ]   sends faxes   [   ]

Now read the article and check your answers.

Reprinted with permission from WORKING WOMAN magazine. Copyright © 1991 by W. W. T. Partnership

Managers: Do you type too much?

A study of 1500 employees in top American companies shows that managers spend only about a quarter of their time managing. What do they do the *rest* of their time? Clerical work.

"In many organizations management tries to pay for computer systems by getting rid of clerical staff," says Peter Sassone, an economist at the Georgia Institute of Technology in Atlanta. But computer systems cannot do the work of secretaries, so managers spend a lot of their time faxing, filing and opening the mail.

How to solve the problem? If organizations cannot afford to hire extra staff, it's time to cut down on paperwork, says Sassone. For example, write some reports less often – or not at all. It's also a good idea to invest in a day or two of training so that you learn what your software can do.

Clerical Staff

Managers

Source of information in picture: Ricoh Corporation

Read the article again. Are these sentences true [T] or false [F]?

1 Managers spend 25% of their time on clerical work.   [   ]
2 If you have a good computer, you don't need a secretary. [   ]
3 13% of managers send faxes very often.   [   ]
4 48% of clerical staff photocopy very often.   [   ]
5 Many managers need to go on a computer course.   [   ]

What else does a manager do?

B Match the request with a suitable response.

1 Could you make a copy of this report?
2 Would you type this letter? It's rather urgent.
3 Could you meet Mr Ramone at the airport for me?
4 Could you phone Ms Taylor about the new brochures?
5 Would you make some more coffee?
6 Could you work on Saturday?

A Sure. Black with sugar?
B Of course. What's her extension?
C I'm rather busy right now. Can I type it tomorrow?
D I'd rather not. It's my birthday.
E No problem. What time is he arriving?
F Sure.

Listen and check your answers. Then practise the conversations.

C Work in pairs. Ask your partner to do some things. Student A looks at File 9 on page 118 and Student B looks at File 10 on page 120.

D Listen to these phone calls. Is the information on the confirmation faxes correct?

1 Could you please send brochures on your courses for executive secretaries?

Our address is:

140 Canal Road
Meriden
Connecticut 06540

2 Could you reserve a single room with shower at the Crown Hotel for Mr Axelsson from 20 – 23 June?

3 Could you send 5000 pieces, ref. no F110 to the factory as soon as possible?

7.2 Talking about stress

A Make sentences with words in the table. Then compare them with a partner's.

| A manager An engineer A secretary | has to must | do overtime. work long hours. travel a lot. make decisions. |
| | doesn't have to needn't | meet deadlines. prepare reports. go to conferences. |

Make a list of things you <u>have to</u> do. Find out what your partner has to do.

B What makes a job stressful? Read this article to find out.

Is your job making you ill?

The tempo of work, new technology and shift work are the cause of work-related illnesses which cost industry £1.3 bn a year. Company culture is often an important factor. Many employees have to spend long hours at work to get promotion. This is often the case in office jobs where companies expect people to work longer for their basic hours as anything else is disloyal.

Stress creates problems for the individual and the organization. It is a danger to the employee's health, family and social life. But employers often ignore the effects on the work place: absenteeism, poor work and dangerous health and safety factors. When people are tired they make mistakes and mistakes cost money.

C Are you stressed? Do the questionnaire and find out.

1 How many hours a day do you work?

   a) less than 8
   b) 8
   c) more than 8

2 How much time do you spend on holiday each year?

   a) four or more weeks
   b) between two and four weeks
   c) what's a holiday!

3 Do you find time to exercise?

   a) daily
   b) weekly
   c) what's exercise!

4 Do you have time to do all the things you have to do?

   a) always; you're well-organized
   b) sometimes; when things go smoothly
   c) never; you can't manage your time

5 How do you spend your free time?

   a) with family and friends
   b) on your own
   c) behind your desk

6 Do you:

   a) smoke?
   b) drink a lot of coffee?
   c) worry?
   d) get angry easily?
   e) think of changing your job?

Scoring 1–5: a = 1; b = 2; c = 3. Question 6: add one point for every 'yes'.

16–20: You are very stressed. How can you change this?

11–15: You are quite ambitious. Be careful!

6–10: You are fairly relaxed.

0–5: You are not just relaxed, you are almost asleep!

D Listen to this woman talking about her routine. What's her score on the questionnaire?

1 a) b) c)   4 a) b) c)
2 a) b) c)   5 a) b) c)
3 a) b) c)   6 a) b) c) d) e)

Total: ....

7.3 Giving advice

A Look at the pictures. What are Henry Ditheridge's problems?

B What advice can you give Henry? Match the problem to a suitable response.

1 It takes me an hour to get to work.
2 I've got a terrible cough!
3 I don't feel very fit.
4 I'm often at the office until 8.00 pm.
5 I never see my family.
6 I can't stop thinking about work.

A You should stop smoking.
B Take up a hobby.
C Why don't you cycle?
D You should go home from work at 5.00.
E Go for a walk at lunchtime.
F Don't spend every evening with colleagues.

Listen and check your answers. Then practise with a partner.

C Study these examples.

> **Stop** smoking.
> You **should** relax.
> **Why don't you** go on holiday?
> **Don't** smoke.
> You **shouldn't** work so hard.

Here are some more ways of avoiding stress.
Complete the sentences with suitable words.

1 .... work near home.
2 .... watch your watch.
3 .... talk to colleagues.
4 .... drink herbal teas, not coffee?
5 .... laugh.
6 .... leave for appointments at the last minute.
7 .... take all your holidays.
8 .... plant a tree and watch it grow?

D Work in groups. What advice can you give these people?

> I'm always tired.

> It takes me two hours to get to work.

> I can't sleep.

> My colleague smokes non-stop.

> I'm always late for work.

> My boss wants me to learn English.

Compare your advice with another group's. Who has the best ideas?

8 Plans

8.1 Discussing arrangements

A Look at the pictures and match the verbs with the nouns.

1 meet	A a plane
2 attend	B a factory
3 visit	C a meeting
4 have	D a fair
5 catch	E dinner
6 have	F an agent

B 🎧 Listen to Alicia Speld talking about her arrangements for a trip to Singapore and fill in her diary.

Mon	*arrive 17.30*
Tues	
Wed	
Thurs	
Fri	
Sat	
Sun	

C Study these examples.

> **I'm flying** to Singapore **tomorrow**.
> **She's meeting** Mr Lee **on Saturday**.
> **We're catching** the plane **next week**.

Look at Alicia's notes for her trip to Sydney. Match the activities with a time to organize her schedule.

I have to:	Times available:
attend fair	Wednesday afternoon
meet Mr Enrique	Thursday morning
arrive in Sydney	Saturday evening
check into hotel	Tuesday evening
have dinner with agent	Monday afternoon
fly to Melbourne	

Make some sentences like this:

She's arriving in Sydney on Saturday evening.

Compare your sentences with a partner's.

D Read this fax.

Dear Kerry

I'm arriving in Melbourne on Thursday. I'd like very much to see you on Friday to discuss plans for next year. What time on Friday would suit you?

Please let me know as soon as possible.

Regards

Alicia

Write a fax from Kerry to Alicia. Say Friday morning is best.

8.2 Making appointments

A Look at the notes.

> ### Mr Patel's trip
>
> Fly to .... ?
>
> Meet Mr .... ?
>
> Stay at .... Hotel?
>
> Dinner with Mr Smith on .... ?
>
> Go to (1,2,3) meetings?
>
> Stay (2 days, 1 week)?

Use these words to write six questions.

who	when	which	how long	where	how many

Complete the notes with your own information. Then practise asking and answering with a partner.

B Work in pairs. You are going on a business trip to Italy with your partner. Student A looks at File 11 on 116 and Student B looks at File 12 on 119.

C 📼 Listen to Mr Singh arranging a meeting. Write the appointment in the diary.

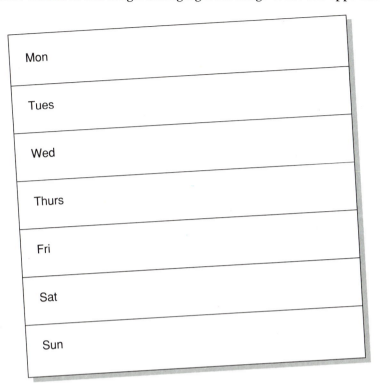

Mon

Tues

Wed

Thurs

Fri

Sat

Sun

D Write down your arrangements for next week. Then phone your partner to arrange a meeting.

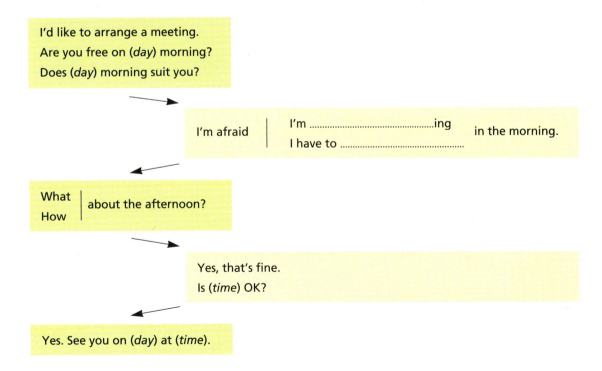

I'd like to arrange a meeting.
Are you free on (*day*) morning?
Does (*day*) morning suit you?

I'm afraid | I'm ....ing in the morning.
I have to ....

What | about the afternoon?
How

Yes, that's fine.
Is (*time*) OK?

Yes. See you on (*day*) at (*time*).

8.3 Planning a trip

A Frank Shaw, an American businessman, is planning a trip to Europe next October. He has to:

go to the Leipzig fair (3 days).
meet Andrea Kovacs in Budapest (half a day).
visit Jiri Svarc in Prague (1 day).

When can he do these things? Study the documents and fill in the possible times on his schedule on the page opposite.

Arrive Prague: 09 October
Depart Prague: 19 October

LEIPZIG FAIR
OCTOBER 06 – 20

PRICE INTERNATIONAL INC

August 16, 199-

Jiri Svarc
Nedvezská, 27
Prague

30 Elm Street
Lakewood
Connecticut 80215
Tel +1 303 232-9696
Fax +1 303 233-5869

Dear Jiri

I'm planning a trip to Europe in October and would like to meet you to discuss opening an office in Prague. I hope to be in Prague on October 17 and 18. Would it be convenient to visit you on Friday, October 18 at 10 a.m.?

I look forward to seeing you.

Regards

Frank

Bebczur Utca 31, 1108 Budapest, Hungary

30 Elm Street
Lakewood
Connecticut 80215

26 August 199-

Dear Mr Shaw

Thank you for your letter of 16 August about your visit to Europe. Unfortunately, I am away until 11 October, but I would be happy to see you on either Monday, 14 or Wednesday, 16 October. Please let me know which day suits you best.

I look forward to your reply.

Sincerely

Andrea Kovacs

09 Wed ....

10 Thurs ....

11 Fri ....

12 Sat ....

13 Sun ....

14 Mon ....

15 Tues ....

16 Wed ....

17 Thurs ....

18 Fri ....

19 Sat ....

B Frank also wants to do these things:

meet Frank Rieger in Dresden (1 day)
meet Witold Wadja in Warsaw (2 days)
spend 2 or 3 days in Prague.

When can he do this? Fill in the times on his schedule. Then compare your timetable
with a partner's.

C ▢ Listen to Frank Shaw phoning another agent, Gabor Dombradi.
When do they arrange to meet?

Now finalize the schedule.

D You are Frank Shaw. Write a short letter to Witold Wadja to arrange a meeting. You want to
discuss a possible agency agreement. Ask him to reserve a hotel room. Address your letter to:

Witold Wadja
Kielecka 30
02 – 530 Warsaw 12
Poland

9 Visits and travel

9.1 Talking to a visitor

A A visitor is coming to your company. It is your first meeting. What can you talk about?

| journey | family | weather | business | hotel | politics |

B 🔲 Listen to Ms Rufer talking to a visitor. What do they talk about? Is this their first meeting? Listen again and fill in the gaps.

Rufer: Hello, Mr Harris.
Harris: Hello.
Rufer: Nice to see you again! .... (1)?
Harris: Oh, not too bad, thanks.
Rufer: And did you arrive .... (2)?
Harris: Yes, by .... (3) from Brussels.
Rufer: Did you have a good .... (4)?
Harris: No, not really. The train was .... (5) and it was very
        .... (6).
Rufer: Oh, I'm sorry to hear that. Were you in Brussels on business?
Harris: Yes, I was at a .... (7). Unfortunately, I didn't have time to look
        round the city. Next time, perhaps.
Rufer: Yes, Brussels is a very nice city. Now, can I get you anything? .... (8)?
Harris: Yes, thank you. That would be nice.

C Study these examples.

Was the train crowded?   **Did** you have a good journey?

Yes, it **was**.   Yes, I **did**.

No, it **wasn't**.   No, I **didn't**.

Were you there on business?

Yes, I **was**.

No, I **wasn't**.

Complete the conversations and practise them with a partner.

1 .... you have a good flight?

   Yes, thank you. Very good. The service .... excellent.

2 .... there a lot of people on the plane?

   No, there .... It .... crowded.

3 .... you in Frankfurt on business?

   No, I .... I .... there with my family.

4 What .... the weather like in Frankfurt?

   Terrible. It .... foggy and cold.

5 .... you have something to eat on the plane?

   Yes, I ....

D Work in pairs. Look at the dialogue in B again. With a partner make as many changes as possible to the dialogue.

9.2 Attending business events

A Do you ever go to any of these business events?

seminar	trade fair
conference	meeting
exhibition	training course

Here are some adjectives to describe them.

Which are positive and which are negative?

interesting	stressful
successful	terrible
disappointing	useful
tiring	productive

Think of the last business event you went to. What was it like?

B Listen to these sentences. How many words do you hear?
(Words like *wasn't* are two words.)

1 ....   4 ....

2 ....   5 ....

3 ....   6 ....

Listen again. Write down the sentences.

C Complete the conversations and practise them.

1 How was the fair?
   We didn't make any new contacts. It was ....

2 Was it a good conference?
   Yes, it was. I think it was very ....

3 How was the exhibition?
   There was a lot to do. It was ....

4 What was the course like?
   It was very hard work. It was ....

5 How was the meeting?
   We were very pleased. I think it was very ....

6 Did you enjoy the seminar?
   We didn't learn anything new. It wasn't very ....

D 📼 Listen to Sarah, Isobel and Pedro talking about recent business events.
Who went:

> to a trade fair?
> on a training course?
> to a conference?

Listen again. Who said what?

1 There was an excellent atmosphere.
2 Tiring!
3 There simply wasn't enough time to talk to everyone.
4 The hotel was fantastic.
5 My hotel was a bit far out.
6 Our stand was really crowded.
7 It was nice to be out of the office for a few days.
8 We made a lot of good contacts.
9 I learnt a lot.

9.3 Reserving a hotel room

A   Read the descriptions of three hotels in Bangkok. <u>Underline</u> the facilities or services.

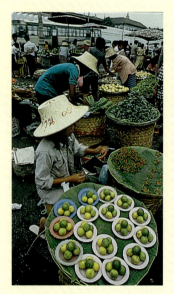

All rooms in the hotels have air conditioning, 24 hour room service, TV, radio and most have IDD (international direct dialing) phones. Other facilities include photocopying, typing, telex, fax and translation.

1 . . . .   **2** . . . .   **3** . . . .

This large hotel offers business people excellent facilities including interpreters and computer hire. It has a large pool and a wide range of sporting and leisure events.

Tower complex with a big shopping arcade; business and sports centre, a wide choice of bars and restaurants; ideal for sales conferences.

In a quiet location, close to the central business district. The business centre is open daily. Shops, hairdresser, florist, large pool, sauna, fitness centre, tennis, 12 meeting rooms.

Put the facilities in two groups like this:

WORK	LEISURE
Photocopying	TV

Which hotel do you think is best for a business person?

B   Listen to Mr Harada asking for information about hotels in Bangkok.
Write the names of the hotels in the correct place above the photographs on the previous page.

     The Ambassador   The Regent   The Sheraton

C   Work in groups of three. Your company needs a hotel for a conference. You have information about three different hotels. Student A looks at File 13 on page 120, Student B at File 14 on page 118 and Student C at File 15 on page 116.

D   You are going to Frankfurt on business. Write a letter to the Frankfurt Tourist Office and ask them to send you information on hotels in the central business district with these services:

     telefax
     computer hire
     conference room

Address your letter to:

The Frankfurt Tourist Office
Opernstr. 1
6000 Frankfurt/Main 1
Germany

'Work hard, play hard! That's my motto! Another drink?'

UNIT

10 Revision and consolidation

A What do you say? Match the function to the actual words.

1	Talk about your routine.	A	You should take a holiday.
2	Suggest a time for a meeting.	B	Did you have a good journey?
3	Talk about arrangements.	C	Could you make some coffee?
4	Ask about a journey.	D	Would you like a cup of coffee?
5	Give advice.	E	I'm going to Head Office next week.
6	Ask someone to do something.	F	It was a very successful fair.
7	Talk about a business event.	G	Are you free at 12?
8	Offer someone a drink.	H	We usually have a meeting on Fridays.

Work in pairs. Write a short dialogue with some of the phrases above.

B Vocabulary Match the verb in column A with a word in column B.

1	open	A	a company
2	make	B	a report
3	visit	C	a visitor
4	go to	D	a photocopy
5	go on	E	late
6	work	F	the mail
7	write	G	the filing
8	send	H	a fax
9	do	I	a meeting
10	meet	J	a business trip

How often do you do these things? Do you like doing them?
What other words can you use with the verbs?

C Reading

1 Read the article about Andrew Long and complete the information.

Job title: ....

Salary: ....

Age: ....

The Green Accountant

Andrew Long spends about half his time in the office, half out with clients.

....(1)

Andrew, 33, is an environmental auditor at one of Britain's biggest accountancy firms.

....(2)

It is his job to help a company understand its environmental performance. This can mean looking at the energy efficiency of its branches, for example, or its arrangements for waste disposal.

....(3)

In an average week Andrew sees two or three clients. He spends the rest of the time in the office preparing reports, presentations or for conferences.

....(4)

Andrew is paid £40,000 for his know how and long hours; he usually works from nine to nine and six days a week. He has to write his reports in the evenings, out of phone hours, because as soon as he gets to the office the phone starts and goes on most of the day.

....(5)

His job is very stressful, but he enjoys it.

....(6)

2 These sentences are missing. Where do they go?

[ ]   A typical audit for a client takes about three months.
[ ]   He also attends a lot of meetings.
[ ]   As a manager of the environmental business unit, he is responsible for a team of eight.
[ ]   He goes to conferences two or three times a year.
[ ]   But he prefers being out with clients.
[ ]   "It's addictive, you get some real highs."

D 📼 **Listening** Listen to Andrew explaining his schedule for the next month to his boss. Complete his month planner.

	Mo	Tu	We	Th	Fr	Sa	Su
					1	2	3
	4	5	6	7	8	9	10
	Dentist 11	12	13	14	15	16	17
	18	19	20	21	Day off 22	23	24
	Public holiday 25	26	27	28	29	30	31

E Speaking Play this game with a partner.

Mr Murphy, from Los Angeles, is coming to your country and wants to visit your company.

Play with a coin:
Heads – move one square;
Tails – move two squares.

Have conversations with your partner on each square.

START

1 Phone Mr Murphy to arrange a meeting on Tuesday, 21st.

2 Mr Murphy is busy on Tuesday, 21st. Suggest another day.

Mr Murphy asks you about hotels in your town. Recommend one.

20 The phone rings. A customer wants to arrange a meeting for next week. Find a time and miss a turn.

21 Ask Mr Murphy a question.

22 Mr Murphy asks you about your plans for next week. Tell him three things you have to do.

2 Ask Mr Murphy about his plans for the rest of the trip.

19 Mr Murphy asks you about the last fair. Tell him.

18 Mr Murphy wants a copy of the Sales Report. Ask your secretary to make one.

17 Your assistant comes to your office. Introduce him/her to Mr Murphy.

16 You have to make an urgent phone call. Miss a turn.

1 Mr Murphy asks you about your job. Tell him about a typical day.

4 ou can't meet Mr urphy at the airport. iss a turn.

5 Mr Murphy arrives at your office. Greet him.

6 Ask Mr Murphy about his journey.

7 Ask Mr Murphy about the weather in L.A.

8 Offer Mr Murphy something to drink.

24 he phone rings gain. Go back to 20.

25 Your meeting with Mr Murphy was very successful. Well done! Say goodbye to him.

FINISH

9 The phone rings for your colleague. Answer it and miss a turn.

10 Ask your secretary to make some coffee for you and Mr Murphy.

14 sk Mr Murphy three uestions about his ompany.

13 A colleague comes to your office. He feels terrible. Give him some advice and miss a turn.

12 Ask Mr Murphy three questions about working times in the States.

11 It is Mr Murphy's first visit to your country. Tell him about working times.

Work history

11.1 Finding someone a job

A Read this letter from Alain Le Blanc and Patrick Milligan's notes. Are there any mistakes in his notes? Is there anything missing?

WEIL ENGINEERING
41 Rue de l'Ilberg, 68200 Mulhouse, France

Mr Milligan
33 Mountjoy Road
Dublin 1
Ireland

3 April 199-

Dear Patrick

I wonder if you could help me. A colleague of mine, Brigitte O'Brian, is moving to Dublin and looking for a job.

This is her background: She left school in 1980 and trained as a clerk at ABC Pharmaceuticals. She finished her training in 1982 and worked at this company for 4 years. In 1988 she joined our company as a senior clerk. After 2 years she became assistant manager of the export department. In the evenings she took computing and language courses. She now speaks fluent English and some Spanish. Her husband is from Dublin and she lived there for a year in 1987. She is a very good worker and I can recommend her.

If you need any further information, I can ask her to send a complete c.v.

Thank you for your help.

Best wishes

Alain.

---

experience
    1980-82: trainee clerk / ABC Pharmaceuticals
    1982-86: junior clerk / Weil Engineering
    1988-90: senior clerk / Weil Engineering
    1990-now: manager of export department
other information
    Lived in Dublin for 2 years
    Speaks French, English, some Spanish.

B Study these examples.

REGULAR VERBS	IRREGULAR VERBS
I **trained** as a clerk.	She **left** school 5 years ago.
He **finished** his training 3 years ago.	She **became** assistant manager in 1990.
She **worked** there for 3 years.	I **took** an English course last year.

📼 The verbs in the box are all regular, but you say them differently in the past tense. Listen to the verbs in their past tense form and put them in the correct column.

live	pass	need	work	plan	stop	move
ask	attend	study	represent	train	help
want	visit

/d/	/t/	/id/
lived	passed	needed
....	....	....
....	....	....
....	....	....
....	....	....

C 📼 Listen to Jiro Mitsuhashi talking about his career. Complete the notes.

Education and qualifications
....
....
Experience
....
....
Other information
....
....

D Jiro wants to go to the States for a year. You know a businesswoman in New York. Use your notes to write a letter to your friend in New York to ask if she can help Jiro find a job.

Start your letter like this:

3 April 199–

Dear Helen,

I would like to know if you could help me. A friend of mine, Jiro Mitsuhashi, is planning to go to New York for a year and is looking for a job.

This is his background:

Finish your letter like this:

I would be grateful if you could help in this matter.

Best wishes

11.2 Talking about your career

A Match the questions to the answers.

1 When did you join the Cocoa Bean Company?   A 4 years.
2 Which department did you work in?   B Yes, I did.
3 What was your position?   C Production.
4 Did you enjoy it?   D Assistant Production Manager.
5 How long did you stay there?   E I went to America.
6 Why did you leave?   F 10 years ago.

Listen and check your answers.

B Work in pairs. Student A looks at File 16 on page 121 and Student B at File 17 on page 117. You will find some information about two people who work in advertising.

C Make notes on your career: education, training and work experience.
Don't forget any holiday or part-time jobs.

Now find out as much as possible about your partner's career. Don't forget to take notes!
You can ask questions like these:

When did you leave school?
What did you do after that?
What did you do next?

Use your notes to tell others about your partner.

11.3 Describing your first job

A When you talk about past jobs, you often say if you liked a job or not and you give the reason why.

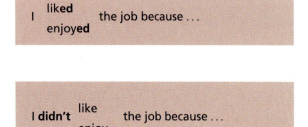

I   lik**ed**   the job because ...
    enjoy**ed**

I **didn't**   like   the job because ...
           enjoy

Write next to each reason whether you think it is describing a good job (+) or a bad job (–).

1 I did a lot of overtime.   [   ]
2 I learnt a lot.   [   ]
3 It was very hard work.   [   ]
4 It was badly paid.   [   ]
5 I worked with interesting people.   [   ]
6 We had flexitime.   [   ]
7 I didn't have much contact with my colleagues.   [   ]
8 The work wasn't very interesting.   [   ]
9 I didn't have much holiday.   [   ]
10 There was an excellent canteen.   [   ]
11 I got on very well with my boss.   [   ]
12 I worked shifts.   [   ]

B Listen to Veronique and Daniela talking about their first jobs.
Fill in the missing information.

Veronique

Position: ....

Responsibilities: *Take dictation* ......
                  Write reports ....

Other information ....
                  ....

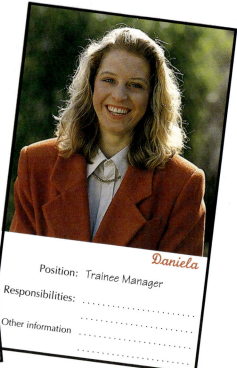

Daniela

Position: Trainee Manager

Responsibilities: ....
                  ....

Other information ....
                  ....

C Find out about your partner's first job and make notes. Ask questions like these:

Who did you work for?
What did you do?
Did you have to work hard?
How much holiday did you get?
Did you enjoy your job?

Tell others about your partner's first job.

12 Fairs and sales

12.1 Finding out about a trade fair

A Read the advertisement for trade fairs in Taipei and find a fair for the products below.

TAIPEI	**The hot word in trade shows**
Taipei Int'l Elec	Mar 01-05
Taipei Int'l Food Industry Show	Mar 12-16
Taipei Int'l Industrial Machinery Show	Apr 06-12
Taipei Int'l Cycle Show	Apr 20-24
Taipei Int'l Auto Show	May 14-18
Computer Taipei	Jun 06-12
Taipei Tech	Jun 21-25
Taipei Import Fair	Aug 26-30
Taipei Int'l Toy Show	Sep 26-30
Taipei Int'l Electronics Show	Oct 13-19
Taipei Int'l Gift and Stationery Show	Oct 26-30
Taipei Fashion Week	Nov 09-13

To find out more about heating up your business, just write to us for information.

Organiser: China External Trade Development Council
Sponsor: Taipei World Trade Centre
5 Hsinyi Road, Sec. 5, Taipei 10509, Taiwan
Tel: (02)725-1111
Fax: 886-2-725-1314
Telex: 28094 TPEWTC

1 ....

2 ....

3 ....

4 ....

5 ....

6 ....

B 🎞 Cycles Unlimited has a stand at the International Cycle Show in Taipei. Listen to Wendy Gordon ringing the Carlton Hotel to arrange accommodation. What is the problem?

C Study these examples.

I need	three single rooms.
	some accommodation.

Are these words countable [C] or uncountable [U]?

1 accommodation	[u]	2 room	[c]	3 job	[ ]	4 work	[ ]
5 information	[ ]	6 details	[ ]	7 dollars	[ ]	8 money	[ ]
9 suitcase	[ ]	10 baggage	[ ]	11 journey	[ ]	12 travel	[ ]

SOME

There is **some** accommodation at the Conference Centre.

There are **some** rooms at the InterCity.

ANY

Have you got **any** accommodation for tonight?

We haven't got **any** single rooms.

<u>Underline</u> the correct word in *italics*. Then practise the conversations with a partner.

1 I'd like *an/some* information about hotels.
   What exactly do you need to know?

2 I'd like to book *an/some* accommodation. Have you got *some/any* single rooms for tonight?
   I'm sorry, but we haven't got *some/any* single rooms.

3 Are there *some/any* good restaurants near the hotel?
   I'm afraid not. But there are *some/any* excellent restaurants near the World Trade Centre.

4 Have you got *some/any* luggage?
   Yes, it's over there.

5 I haven't got *some/any* money.
   Don't worry. I've still got *some/any* dollars.

D Work in pairs. You want to book some accommodation for the International Cycle Show. Student A looks at File 18 on page 116 and Student B looks at File 19 on page 120.

12.2 Talking about products

A Match the pictures to the product description.

cycles

cycle helmet

cycle bags

cycle computer

mountain bike

shoe

1 .... for the future. Italian frame and Japanese components. Standard model: $1599. Deluxe model: $1899. Available in green and yellow.

2 Easy to use .... with large display. Functions: trip time – trip distance – speed – average speed – clock – temperature. $139.

3 The ideal .... for both long and short cycle tours. Man-made soles, leather uppers. Available in white or grey. Sizes 37-47. $109.

4 All-purpose range of .... This budget range is manufactured in nylon with a choice of two fashionable colours. $159.

5 Classic range with a high-tech image. This .... is suitable for all ages. $399.

6 The safety .... for young cyclists. Suitable for children from 6 years. Colours: white. Weight: 225g. $59.

Read the descriptions again and <u>underline</u> the words and expressions which helped you get the answers.

B 🔲 Listen and say these prices.

1 US$69.50	6 £199
2 HK$109	7 DM15,99
3 Pta 159	8 FF100
4 A$259	9 ¥500
5 SwF1899	10 Lit 1500

What other currencies are there?

C [cassette icon] Listen to a customer asking for information about mountain bikes at a trade fair. Which two bicycles do they talk about?

1 $159

2 $159

3 $239

4 $199

D Study these examples.

This is our (*model*).	It costs (*price*).
It's suitable for (*purpose*).	We can deliver (*from stock*).
It's available in (*colour*) and (*size*).	We can offer a discount of (*%*).

You work for a sportswear company. Look at the pictures and complete the table with information about one of your products.

Suitable for: ....

Colours: ....

Sizes: ....

Price: ....

Discount: ....

Find out about your partner's product and make notes on what you find out. Ask questions like these:

Is it suitable for… ?
What colours is it available in?
How much is it? / What's the retail price?
When can you deliver?
Can you give me a discount?

Tell the others about your partner's product. Is it a good buy?

12.3 Placing an order

A Look at the order form. Where can you write details about the things in the box?

discount   delivery   number of goods   payment
type of goods   cost of one item

Waters Sportswear, 12 Chandos St., St Leonards, NSW 2065 Australia

Order No. AB 2371

Mr Peter Sung
Del Mar Sporting Ltd
181 Tras Street # 07-177
Singapore 0207

10 September 199–

Quantity	Description of Goods	Unit Price	Total
		Total amount	

Comments:

Authorized by

....

(International ++61-2)   Tel. 438-6351   Fax. 438-7025

B Listen to Colin Hirst phoning Del Mar Sporting Ltd and complete the order form.

C Use the information on the order form to complete this letter.

....

....

....

....

....

....

....

Dear ....

We enclose our .... AB 2371 for the following:

....

....

....

We would like to confirm that .... is by letter of credit. Thank you for the .... of 10%.

We would appreciate .... within the next 6 weeks and look forward to receiving your acknowledgement.

Yours sincerely

Colin Hirst

13 Product description

13.1 Comparing products

A Look at these two advertisements for a notebook and desktop computer.

Save, save, save!

*1 year warranty.
*1-day free training.
*Free 24-hour delivery.
*Technical support on our hot line - call anytime in business hours.
*14-day money-back guarantee.
*On-site maintenance contract only $50!
*$350 software package - free!

Buy now, only $1550 ! !

$1250

What a bargain!

*12-month warranty.
*48-hour home delivery.
*30-day money-back guarantee.
*Free on-site maintenance.
*Software worth $150 included in the package.
*2 days free training at our company.

Come & see our wide range of computers & printers

1 What do these figures refer to?

A 1 year	E $350 ....
B $1250	F 1-day ....
C 48-hour	G 30-day ....
D $50	

2 Are these sentences true [T] or false [F]?

A The notebook is cheaper than the desktop. [ ]
B The notebook has a longer warranty than the desktop. [ ]
C The notebook has a shorter delivery time than the desktop. [ ]
D The notebook has better technical support than the desktop. [ ]
E The notebook has a longer money-back guarantee. [ ]
F Maintenance for the notebook is more expensive. [ ]
G The notebook's on-site service is not as cheap as the desktop's. [ ]
H You get less training with the notebook. [ ]

3 Listen and mark the stress on these words.

1 warranty   4 delivery
2 guarantee   5 technical
3 installation

B Study these examples and then correct the false sentences in A.

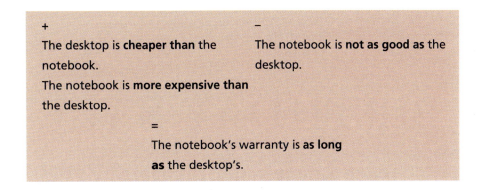

+
The desktop is **cheaper than** the notebook.
The notebook is **more expensive than** the desktop.

–
The notebook is **not as good as** the desktop.

=
The notebook's warranty is **as long as** the desktop's.

C Work in pairs. Imagine your company sells photocopiers. Make a short advertisement for one of your photocopiers.

Include details about:

warranty   contract
delivery time   price
on-site service   money-back guarantee

Compare your product with another pair. What is the same and what is different?

13.2 Saying what's best

A 🔲 Listen to the radio commercial for Computer World and match the adjectives on the left with the nouns on the right.

1	big	A	computers
2	wide	B	selection
3	low	C	sale
4	modern	D	prices
5	large	E	range
6	good	F	service

B Study these examples and then complete the advertisement with suitable words.

ADJECTIVE	COMPARATIVE	SUPERLATIVE
cheap	cheap**er**	cheap**est**
large	larg**er**	larg**est**
big	big**ger**	big**gest**
expensive	**more** expensive	**most** expensive
good	better	best

BIRTHDAY SALE!!!

Office Supply's 10th Anniversary sale.

Yes, it's our birthday but YOU get the presents!

It's the best offer in town! Come to **Office Supply** for the .... prices, the .... service and the .... equipment for the office. We have everything from computers to furniture. We have the .... range of telefaxes in the city and the .... selection of office furniture. We're open longer hours than other shops, so come to us. We're the ....! Don't forget the .... thing – if it's office equipment you need, then you need

OFFICE SUPPLY

🔲 Listen and check your answers.

C You are interested in the laser printer, the Easyprint II. Is Office Supply really the best place to buy office equipment?

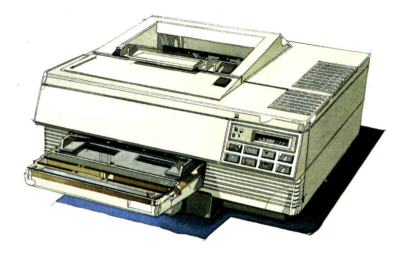

1 [cassette] Listen to the telephone conversation between a caller and Office Supply, and fill in the details:

> ## Easyprint II
>
> Price:
> Warranty:
> Service contract:
> Money-back guarantee:
> Delivery:

2 Work in pairs. Student A looks at File 20 on page 118 and Student B looks at File 21 on page 121. You will roleplay a conversation between the caller and another supplier.

3 Which is the best place to buy the printer? Make some sentences and then discuss the offers with a partner.

Office Supply Crazy Joe Hobsons	is has	the cheapest the most expensive the lowest the highest the longest the shortest the fastest the best the worst	price. delivery time. warranty. service conditions. money-back guarantee. offer.

13.3 Making suggestions

A Can you name the things in the office?

What do you need in an office? Complete the chart with the items in the picture like this:

ESSENTIAL	QUITE IMPORTANT	NOT IMPORTANT
desk		

Compare your answers with a partner like this:

> *I think a computer is more important than a typewriter.*
> *In my opinion telex isn't as useful as fax.*

B Study these examples.

MAKING SUGGESTIONS

Let's *buy some new chairs.*

I think we should
have a coffee machine.
We could

Put the dialogue in the right order.

Yes. How about some pictures on the wall, too?	[ ]
That's a good idea. We can put the files up there.	[ ]
This office is awful. There's no room to put anything anywhere.	[1]
I agree. I think we should get executive chairs.	[ ]
Good idea. But perhaps we should speak to Mr Austin first.	[ ]
These chairs are really uncomfortable.	[ ]
And we could get some plants.	[ ]
Let's buy a bookcase.	[ ]

Listen and check your answers.

C You are moving to a new office with two colleagues. Make a list of the things you need. You have $10,000 to spend.

OFFICE FURNITURE

DESKS	
– standard size	$300
– large size	$400

TABLES	
– office table	$100
– reception table	$100

STORAGE	
– filing cabinet	$300
– cupboard	$250
– bookcase	$80

SEATING	
– armchair	$100
– typist	$200
– executive	$500
– sofa	$250

COFFEE AND TEA MACHINE	$120

FRIDGE	$350

OFFICE EQUIPMENT

TYPEWRITERS	
– manual	$150
– electronic	$325

PHOTOCOPIERS	
– black and white	$1000
– colour	$2000

TELEPHONE	
– standard	$100
– with answering machine	$300
– cordless	$500

FAX	$600

TELEX	$1200

COMPUTERS	
– notebook	$3500
– desktop	$2000

TELEVISION	$250

Talk about your list with your two new colleagues. Decide together what you need.

14 Entertaining

14.1 Taking a guest to dinner

A Look at the pictures. Do you think these people are friends, colleagues or business partners?

B Look at what these people say about customs in their countries. What is the same in your country?

> We rarely invite guests to our home.
> We usually give a dinner in a restaurant.

> You shouldn't be surprised if you invite a local businessman and his wife to dinner and only the man comes.

> It's common for businesswomen to accept invitations to dinner and to entertain on their own.

> In my country it is impolite to discuss business at lunch unless your host introduces the topic.

c Look at these sentences. Do you think they are true [T] or false [F]?

1 It's often difficult for American women to invite their business partners to dinner. [   ]
2 It's very important to see your business partners socially. [   ]
3 Businessmen enjoy playing sports with women. [   ]
4 If you see a woman with a man in a restaurant it can't be business. [   ]
5 Business lunches are often difficult to arrange. [   ]
6 You should never take your business partners to the same restaurants as your colleagues. [   ]

Now read this article by an American businesswoman and see if you are right.

This Working Life

by Maureen Dowd

In the world of business, it is not always easy for women to do the same things as men. Consider the working dinner.

In order to do your job well, it's important to sometimes see clients and business contacts away from the office. In a more relaxed atmosphere, you can get to know your business partner better. In the end, after all, people do business with people they like.

Women start out at a disadvantage because, unless you're Nancy Lopez or Martina Navratilova, it's tough to invite men out for a game of golf or tennis. Men usually prefer to play sports with other men.

You might think that restaurants are the perfect playing field. But they can be dangerous ground. If people from the office see two men they know having dinner together, they think it's business. If colleagues see a woman dining with a man, they often wonder if it's another kind of business.

I'm still looking for the perfect solution. Breakfasts are out because I find it impossible to be pleasant at 7 AM over a bowl of muesli. I love lunching, but that's usually a bad time for busy people, especially if they are on the road. So that brings us back to dinner.

One answer is to take another colleague or client to the dinner so that no one can think it is a tête-à-tête. Of course, this isn't always convenient. So when I can't do this, I take guys out to dinner one-on-one – to places where I'm most likely to see colleagues. The more your colleagues see you doing working dinners with different men, the more they know it is part of your business style.

"I'll have the businesswoman's lunch."

Read the article again. Do you agree with the writer's opinions?
Compare your answers with a partner's.

14.2 Making invitations

A  Christine Grimes wants to invite Mr Ernst, a customer, to lunch to discuss her company's latest product. You will hear two versions of the telephone call. Which one is more polite and friendly?

B Work in pairs. Practise this dialogue with a partner.

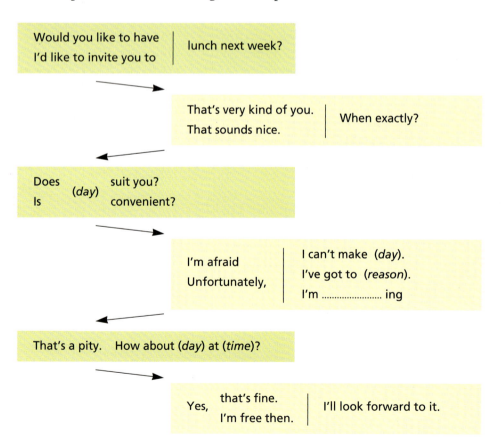

| Would you like to have | lunch next week? |
| I'd like to invite you to | |

| That's very kind of you. | When exactly? |
| That sounds nice. | |

| Does | (day) | suit you? |
| Is | | convenient? |

I'm afraid	I can't make (day).
Unfortunately,	I've got to (reason).
	I'm .... ing

| That's a pity.   How about (day) at (time)? |

| Yes, | that's fine. | I'll look forward to it. |
| | I'm free then. | |

C Work in pairs. Invite your partner to lunch next week. Student A looks at File 24 on page 117 and Student B looks at File 25 on page 119.

D Mr Cheok receives this letter from a business associate in Belgium.
What has Mr Cheok arranged?

MAYTEX Europe N.V.,
Dorpstraat 19,
3030 Leuven,
Belgium.

Tel. (32) 016-202065
Fax (32) 016-202074

Mr Cheok
Block X/4 Kav No. 10
Jalan H R Rasuna Said
Kuningan, Jakarta 12950
Indonesia

12 August 199-

Dear Mr Cheok

Thank you for your letter of 18 July. It would be a great
pleasure to meet you on 10 October at the fair in Brussels.

On the evening of 11 October our company is having a reception at
the Hilton Hotel and I would be very pleased if you could attend.

I look forward to hearing from you soon.

Yours sincerely

A. de Haan

A. de Haan

European Manager

Unfortunately, Mr Cheok has another arrangement for 11 October.
Write a letter to Mr de Haan explaining why he can't come.

14.3 Describing food

A Match the words in the box with the pictures.

aubergine	avocado	bananas	beans	beef	chicken	fish	ice cream
lamb	melon	mushrooms	pasta	prawns	rice	soup	strawberries

1 .... 2 .... 3 .... 4 ....

5 .... 6 .... 7 .... 8 ....

9 .... 10 .... 11 .... 12 ....

13 .... 14 .... 15 .... 16 ....

When do you normally eat these foods? As part of:

  a starter?
  a main course?
  a dessert?

B 🔲 You will hear four short conversations in a restaurant. Match the dish on the left with its description on the right.

1 Schneckensuppe   A dessert
2 Caldeirada   B soup
3 Bagare baingan   C fish
4 Phal mava   D vegetable

C Make a list of food that a visitor to your country would not know. You can describe it like this:

It's a local speciality.

It's very popular here.

It's a kind of vegetable.

It's (a bit) like . . .

It's fairly hot.

It's quite rich.

It's very sweet.

It's quite spicy.

D Work in groups. Some important customers are coming to your company. Plan a menu for them. You should have a starter, a main course and a dessert. Then explain your menu to someone from another group.

Revision and consolidation

A **What do you say?** Match the function to the actual words.

1 Make a suggestion.	A I joined the company two years ago.
2 Refuse an invitation.	B Let's buy a new computer.
3 Ask someone a question about the past.	C This one's more expensive.
	D It's available in three sizes.
4 Ask for information.	E Would you like to join me for lunch on Wednesday?
5 Talk about the past.	F Why did you leave your last job?
6 Compare.	G I'd like some information about flights to Toyko.
7 Talk about a product.	H That's very kind of you, but I'm afraid I can't make
8 Invite someone to lunch.	Wednesday.

Work in pairs. Write a short dialogue with some of the phrases above.

B **Vocabulary** Look at the words in the box and put them into groups.

> discount   starters   arrival   experience
>
> main course   single room   education   qualifications
>
> payment   desserts   departure   quantity

Order Form	Menu	Application	Hotel
....	....	....	....
....	....	....	....
....	....	....	....

Add more words to each group.

....	....	....	....
....	....	....	....
....	....	....	....

C   Reading Read the questionnaire and complete it with the words from the box.

wife	manager	tennis	price	colleagues
color	work life	foreign travel		

SUPERDESK ORGANIZER

Thank you for choosing this quality product from SuperDesk. We are confident that it will give you excellent service. Please fill in this questionnaire – the information will be processed by Consumer Link.

A   About your purchase: We are keen to listen to our customers to learn about their changing needs. Your answers will be a great help to us.

1   If you received your organizer as a gift, who gave it to you?
   [ ] Mother/father   [ ] Husband/................. (1)   [ ] .... (2)
   [ ] Sister/brother   [ ] Other relative   [ ] Other

2   Is this organizer for: (Tick only ONE)
   [ ] .... (3)   [ ] Social life   [ ] Both work and social life

3   Why did you choose a SuperDesk organizer? (Tick no more than TWO)
   [ ] Easily available   [ ] Reputation   [ ] Quality
   [ ] .... (4) [ ] Recommendation   [ ] Other

4   Why did you choose this particular organizer? (Tick no more than TWO)
   [ ] Suitable size   [ ] Right price   [ ] Choice of inserts
   [ ] .... (5) [ ] Product features   [ ] Other

B   About yourself: We would also like to know more about you as a person – it helps us design new products and plan advertising.

5   Occupation
   [ ] Professional   [ ] Clerical   [ ] Student
   [ ] .... (6) [ ] Manual   [ ] Retired
   [ ] Administrator   [ ] Housewife   [ ] Other

6   To help us understand your leisure interests, please tick the activities and interests you enjoy regularly.
   [ ] Cycling   [ ] Eating out   [ ] .... (8)
   [ ] .... (7) [ ] Gardening   [ ] Wildlife
   [ ] Jogging   [ ] Book reading   [ ] Current affairs
   [ ] Walking   [ ] Music   [ ] Science/technology
   [ ] Golf   [ ] Theater/cinema   [ ] Other

D   [cassette] Listening Listen to a market researcher interviewing someone who has just bought a SuperDesk organizer and complete the questionnaire.

E Speaking   Play this game with a partner.

You are going to a trade fair.

Play with a coin:

Heads – move one square.
Tails – move two squares.

Have conversations with your partner on each square.

START

1 Phone the Intercontinental Hotel and book accommodation for you and your colleague.

2 Tell your colleague about the flight:
KLM 223
dep: 09.15
arr: 15.45

3 You arrive at the Intercontinental. Check in.

20 Tell a colleague about the food in your country. Describe a typical dish.

21 Someone asks you about an old colleague. She left your company last year. Tell him/her.

22 Oh dear! Too much to drink! Miss a turn.

2. Give a colleague your name and address.

19 You start talking to someone at the bar. Ask three questions.

18 Tell a colleague something about your company.

17 You go to a bar with some colleagues. Someone asks you what you do. Tell him/her.

16 It's the evening. Phone your boss and tell him/her about your day at the fair.

1 An old customer comes to your stand. What do you say?

4
the first day of the
de fair and you are
e. Miss a turn.

5
A caller wants some
information about
your products:
   suitable for?
   price?
   colours?

6
Find out something
about this caller:
   name?
   company?
   area of interest?

7
A caller wants
information about
your products:
   price?
   guarantee?
   delivery times?

8
It's time for lunch.
Invite your colleague
to have something to
eat with you.

24
u are very tired.
one for a Taxi to
ke you back to your
tel.

25
It's 1am. You arrive
back at your hotel,
but you can't find
your key. What do
you do?

FINISH

9
This caller wants to
know why your
products are better
than the stand next to
you. Tell him/her.

10
A caller places a large
order. Move forward
to 13.

14
caller invites you
ut for a drink after
e fair. Refuse
olitely.

13
You need more
brochures. Miss a turn
while you get some.

12
You have time to
visit another stand.
Ask three questions.

11
Invite a customer for a
drink after the fair
tonight.

87

16 Firms and factories

16.1 Visiting a factory

A What are the people saying? Match the sentences to the pictures.

1
2
3
4
5
6

A Please come this way.
B Could you sign the visitor's book?
C It's a safety requirement to wear this.
D That's it. Is there anything else you'd like to see?
E You need this for security.
F Please be careful.

B 🔊 Listen to Mario Bianchi visiting a factory. Look at the pictures and expressions again and check your answers.

C Look at what you say to warn someone.

> WARNINGS
>
> Watch out.   Please be careful.   Stand back please.
>
>   You have to pay attention to …   Stop.
>
> Don't touch that please.   Get back.
>
>   It's important not to touch the machinery.

What can you say in these situations?

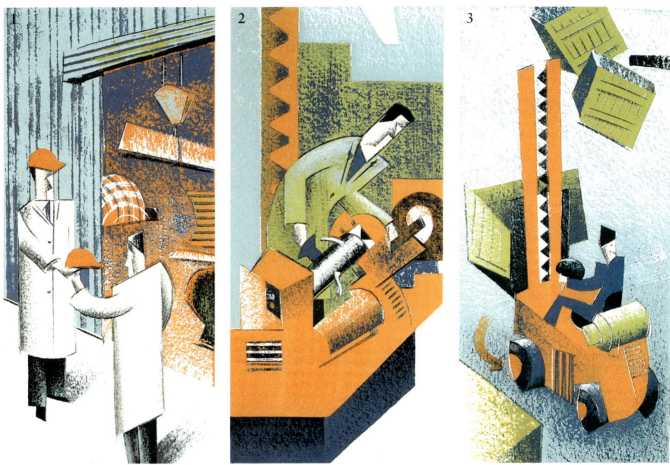

D Work in groups. Draw a plan of your company with the different departments.

Some visitors are coming to spend a day in your company. Which department will you show them? Arrange a day's programme for them. Use your plan as a guide and take a partner on a tour of your company. Use these expressions to help you.

This is the …

In this department we …

Here's the …

This is where we …

16.2 Saying what you've done

A Look at this memo and fill in the verbs.

introduce   show   explain   arrange

internal memo

To: Brian Palmer
From: Diana Steimle
Date: 28 November 199-

Brian

I have to go to London for a couple of days. Mr Bianchi is arriving for training tomorrow. Could you:

1 .... the agenda of the training programme.

2 .... him around the company.

3 .... him to the training manager.

4 .... a meeting with the production manager.

Thank you very much for your help.

Diana

 Listen to Diana Steimle phoning Brian Palmer. What has he done?

B   Look at these examples.

PRESENT PERFECT	PAST SIMPLE
I've (have) explained the agenda.	I visited it **last Monday**.
Have you introduced him to Jon?	He met the staff **yesterday**.
He hasn't arranged a meeting yet.	He went to HQ **last week**.

<u>Underline</u> the correct tense. Then practise the conversations.

1 Have you seen the new company video?
   Yes, I *saw/'ve seen* it yesterday.
2 Have you met the new Personnel Manager yet?
   No, I *just came/'ve just come* back from holiday.
3 Have Deskprint sent us their new brochure?
   Yes, it *arrived/has arrived* last Thursday.
4 Have you read the financial report?
   No, I *didn't have/haven't had* time yet.
5 Have you had lunch yet?
   No, I *was/'ve been* too busy.

C   Work in pairs. Student A looks at File 26 on page 121 and Student B at File 27 on page 122.

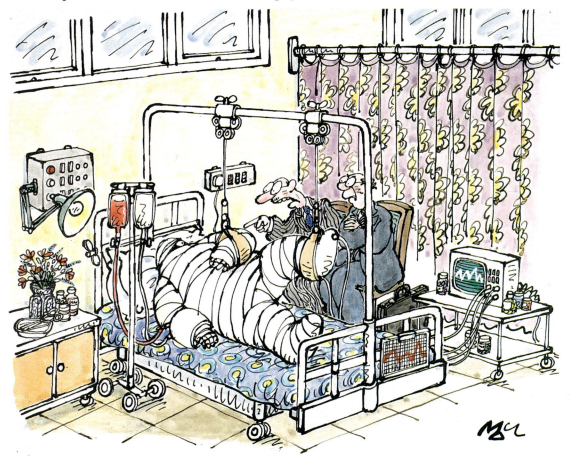

'I hope you finished the accounts before this happened!'

16.3 The company report

A You can often read about some of the topics in the box in company reports. Which ones are mentioned in this report?

sales   personnel   investments   markets

competition   new products   prices   new businesses

OPERATIONS REVIEW

The American Pasta Corporation has had a very successful year. Sales of our major pasta brands have been excellent and sales of private label pasta to retail chains and wholesalers are also up 6% from the previous year.

Consumer response to our new microwave pasta has been disappointing. We have now removed it from the normal distribution channels and plan to market it to consumers as a speciality item.

We sold our major pasta lines to customers for the same price for 5 years. Unfortunately, general business conditions and the cost of packaging material means we have had to increase prices on standard lines. This is the first price increase for five years.

This year we have acquired Rigoletto Pasta Group. *Rigoletto* is the leading brand in the New York metropolitan area, the largest pasta consumption area in the United States. It is also a leading brand in Florida and in several western states.

We have invested in new equipment. In December, we opened a new pasta drying facility. This new system has replaced older systems in the main plant. Additionally, we have installed a new line to manufacture *Al Dente*, the company's leading brand.

Has the American Pasta Corporation had a good year? Read the report again and find some examples of good and bad news.

B You will hear three department managers – a marketing manager, a personnel manager, and a quality control manager – talking about developments in their departments. What subjects in the box do you think each one will talk about?

advertising	English courses	training
market research	employees	costs

Now listen and see if you were right. What else do they say?

C

My boss has left.

Really. When did she leave?

We've opened a new warehouse.

Really. When did you do that?

What has happened in your company? Think about:

employees
equipment
buildings
products and services

Find out your partner's news. Tell the others what you have found out.

17 The Business Pleasure Trip

17.1 Finding out about a city

A Read this article about Chicago and match the headings to the paragraphs.

| transport | theater | restaurants |
| weather | concerts | sightseeing |

1 ....
Chicago is known as the Second City, but for drama it's first-rate. The city has over a hundred professional theaters, where you can see many of America's new writers and actors. Check out the Victory Garden Theater and the Chicago Dramatists' Workshop on the North Side.

2 ....
The Chicago Symphony is world-famous, its Orchestra Hall a fine example of classic architecture. For more funky music, check out B.L.U.E.S. on North Halstead Street and Blues Chicago on North State Street, both convenient to the business district.

3 ....
With its huge eastern European and Mediterranean populations, Chicago is the place for food from the Old World. For German cuisine try Berghoff, located in the Loop (the business and financial district). If you like Greek food, go to Greek Islands or one of the other eateries in Greek town, just west of the Loop. If you want a great view and a meal to match, reserve a window table at the 40th-floor Everest Room in the Loop.

4 ....
Chicago is best seen on foot. Check out the shops on North Michigan Avenue. Take an early morning walk in the parks along Lake Shore Drive. In the summer, you may want to join Chicagoans in a swim in the lake.

5 ....
A car is optional, the subway system is good, and the cabs are relatively inexpensive.

6 ....
A word on the weather: the city's famous winds can cause extreme changes in temperature. Even in the summer there can be 30-degree differences – it can be 90 degrees one day and 60 degrees the next. So bring a sweater.

Read the article again and make some sentences.

If you're interested in If you like	modern music the theatre classical music German food Greek food shopping	you should …

B 〔▭〕 Malcolm Miller is going to a conference in New York next month. Listen to him talking to a colleague about his plans for the weekend. Mark the things they talk about.

Entertainment:
   [ ]   Broadway
   [ ]   Off Broadway

Restaurants:
   [ ]   Greenwich Village
   [ ]   Rainbow Room
   [ ]   Royalton Hotel

Shopping:
   [ ]   Bloomingdale's
   [ ]   Fifth Avenue
   [ ]   Madison Avenue
   [ ]   SoHo

Transport:
   [ ]   cabs
   [ ]   subway
   [ ]   bus
   [ ]   on foot

Listen again. What does his colleague say about each thing?

C Work in groups. Make a list of things that you can tell a visitor about your home town. Include the following and any other things you can think of:

entertainment
restaurants
sightseeing
transport
weather

17.2 Making offers

A 1 Which verbs can go with which nouns?

call		airport
book		hotel
find out about	a	table
reserve	the	taxi
meet you at		seat
pick you up at		tour

2 ☐ Listen to Martine Dubois phone George Sikorski to discuss her trip. **What does George offer to do? Look at the pictures.**

B Study these examples.

OFFERING

Do you want me to get you a taxi?

Shall I book you a hotel?

Would you like me to pick you up?

ACCEPTING	DECLINING
Thank you. That's very kind of you.	No, don't worry.
Yes, please. If it's no trouble.	It's all right, thank you.

What offers can you make?

1 Your visitor needs a hotel room.
2 It's your visitor's first visit to your town.
3 There are tours of the city in the afternoon.
4 Your visitor's very interested in tennis. There's a tennis tournament at the weekend.
5 You know a nice restaurant.
6 Your visitor wants to go to the hotel.

C Look at this extract from *This Month in Bath*. What can you do with a visitor?

The Bath Tour

See the splendour of Georgian Bath from an open top bus on an hour long tour. Departs daily from the Abbey at 10.20 am. Last tour 2.20 pm. Adults £4.00. Children £2.00.

 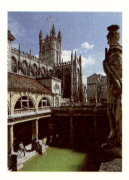

Le Parisien
Cafe by Day

An authentic French establishment in the heart of Bath. Open all day until 10.30 pm. Closed Tuesday nights.

11 Old Bond Street.
Reservations 0225 469999

Sport and Leisure Centre
North Parade Road
(Tel. 462563)
Mon – Sat   8.00 - 10.30 pm.
  Sunday   8.00 - 10.00 pm.

Facilities for swimming, squash, badminton, bowls, table tennis, a sauna, solarium and recreation programmes.

Tel. for details

Bath Antiques Market

Every Wednesday 6.30 am - 2.30 pm
Over 80 dealers make this the largest One Day Market with the widest choice of antiques in the West Country.

Guinea Lane, off Lansdown Road, Bath
Tel 071 351 5353 or 0225 337638

Theatre Royal

LUNCH AND LISTEN
Includes interviews with visiting stars, music and plays.

Lunch from 12.15 pm.
Listen from 1.00 pm.

£3.50 inc. food, £1.00 without.

Box Office: Mon – Sat 10.00 am - 8.00 pm.

Telephone 448844

Work in pairs. Student A is host and Student B is a visitor to Bath.
Student A: find three things to do with your visitor. Ask questions like these:

*Are you interested in **antiques**?*
*Do you like classical **music**?*
*Would you like to **play table tennis**?*

17.3 Thanking

A Read about what a good guest should do in the United States.

THE BREAD AND BUTTER NOTE

Whether you were entertained alone or as a part of a group, handwrite a note of thanks to your host. If you were entertained by a married couple, address the note to both, even if your business relationship is with only one of them.

DO YOU NEED TO RETURN THE INVITATION?

No. But it's nice to do a little more if you had a good time. If, for example, you find your host likes Gershwin, send her a tape or a compact disc. A bunch of herbs from your garden for an enthusiastic cook would also be suitable.

What do you do in your country?

B Match the phrase with a suitable reply.

1 That was a lovely meal.	A Yes, that would be nice.
2 Thank you for arranging that.	B It was a pleasure.
3 I'm afraid I must go.	C Thank you. You too.
4 Have a nice weekend.	D Thank you. I will.
5 Give my regards to Mr Montand.	E I'm glad you enjoyed it.
6 We must have another game soon.	F Is that the time?

Listen and check your answers. Then practise the conversations.

C Look at these two letters of thanks. Which one is to a friend? Which one is to a new business partner?

Howard Joys
109 Jesmond Road,
Newcastle upon Tyne
NE2 1NJ

Hans Weber
Bachmann Spielzeuge
Rohrbacher Str. 38
7740 Triberg
Germany

10 August 199-

Dear Mr Weber

I am writing to thank you for your hospitality during my recent trip to Germany.

It is always very useful to meet one's business partners face to face, and I think we had some interesting discussions.

I look forward to seeing you when you visit Newcastle in September.

Your sincerely

Mark Howard

Howard Joys Ltd
109 Jesmond Road
Newcastle upon Tyne
NE2 1NJ

Peter Wagner
Wagner AG
Wasserwerkstrasse 27
8000 Zürich
Switzerland

1 September 199-

Dear Peter

This is just a short note to thank you for a very pleasant evening while I was in Zürich.

It is always good to see old friends again and it was very useful to exchange ideas.

Please give me a ring the next time you come to Newcastle. Perhaps we can meet for lunch.

Best wishes

Mark

D These two letters are mixed up. Put them in the right order.

Please give me a call next time you are in London. Perhaps we can meet for lunch.

I am writing to thank you for your hospitality during my recent trip to Milan.

This is just a short note to thank you for a very plesant evening while I was in Florence.

I had a most enjoyable time and I think our meetings were very successful.

It is always good to see old friends again and it was interesting to hear your views on the new product.

I look forward to seeing you when you visit London in May.

18 Problems, problems

18.1 Dealing with problems

A Which department is responsible for dealing with each problem?

accounts   order processing   after-sales   dispatch
marketing   sales

1 ....

2 ....

3 ....

4 ....

5 ....

6 ....

B Match the problem to a suitable response.

1 They've forgotten to send a price list
  with the catalogue.
2 This manual's in Japanese!
3 We ordered 100 disks. There's only 50 here.
4 They've sent us B 44s. We ordered P 33s.
5 The photocopier's broken down again.
6 I don't think this invoice is right.

A I'll ask them to send us the English one.
B Don't worry. I've phoned the engineer.
  He's coming this afternoon.
C I'll send them back and get them to
  replace them.
D Oh, it's out of print at the moment.
E I'll phone accounts.
F It's OK. The rest are coming later.

Listen and check your answers. Then practise the conversations.

C Study these examples.

> You make a decision **at** the time of speaking:
> I'**ll (will)** phone the engineer.
> You made an arrangement **before** the time of speaking:
> I'**m seeing** the engineer at 12.00.

Complete these conversations and practise them.

1 Have you phoned accounts about the invoice yet?
  No, I haven't. I .... (*do*) it now.

2 We haven't got any paper for the photocopier.
  I .... (*order*) some.

3 I .... (*meet*) Michele for lunch on Friday. Would you like to join us?
  I'm afraid I can't. I .... (*go*) to Head Office.

4 I can't get the printer to work.
  I .... (*show*) you how to do it.

5 What .... (*you/do*) tomorrow?
  I .... (*check*) my diary.

6 Mr Thomas isn't in today. Would you like to leave a message?
  It's all right. I .... (*try*) again tomorrow.

D It is your first day back at work after a holiday. You find these items on your desk.
What will you do with them? Why?

I'll throw it away.

I'll file it.

I'll give it to ....

I'll phone / write to / send ....

Dear Sir/Madam

Thank you for your enquiry of 14 October about our products. We enclose the information requested.

If there is anything else we can help you with please call our office.

Thank you again for your interest.
Yours sincerely

Marcel Delisse

keting Secretary

Dear Customer

We regret to inform you that we will have to put up our prices by an average of 5% at the end of the year. We are very reluctant to do this but most of our suppliers have put up their prices twice in the last year and we now have to pass on the increases.

Yours sincerely

Too much to read! It's impossible to find time to read today's top business books – and thousands are published each year.
  Not keeping up with those books can be a serious and expensive mistake. Often the ideas they contain are available nowhere else.

But how can you know which ones you should read – or find time to read them?

Fortunately, there's a solution ... Quickread Business Book Summaries. It really works.
  Every month, you receive two or three quick-reading, time-saving summaries of the best new business books. Instead of 200 to 500 pages, the summary is only 8 pages. Instead of taking five, ten or more hours to read, it takes only 15 minutes!

Interested? Join now. Fill in the coupon and mail to

Ms Kientsch has to cancel meeting on Friday. Please ring back on 293 2384 to arrange another time.

Learn FRENCH, SPANISH, GERMAN or ITALIAN in 3.5 weeks

You get a much warmer response when you travel and command more respect in business when you speak another language. Accelerated learning shows that language learning can be fast, effective and enjoyable.

Try it yourself FREE for 15 days. Simply fill in the coupon. If you are not completely satisfied, return the course and you will pay nothing.

Office Supplies phoned re invoice no. 352. They say we haven't paid it yet.

Compare your decisions with a partner.

18.2 Complaining and apologizing

A Read this article about Telephone Manners and complete it with these sentences.

A Never begin your sentences with a *no*.
B I'll see what I can do.
C Here's how we handle that. Please call or write to …
D I'll just check for you.
E I'll put you on hold for a minute. Is that all right.

Reprinted with permission from WORKING WOMAN magazine. Copyright © 1990 by W. W. T. Partnership

A lot of business is lost because of the way customers are treated on the phone. The Telephone Doctor, a company which gives workshops and seminars on how to improve employees' telephoning skills, gives the following advice: Teach your employees the five forbidden phrases – and make sure they never use them.

1 'I don't know.' Say instead .... ,

' ....

2 'We don't (or can't) do that.' Try to offer an alternative or say .... ,

' ....

3 'You must …' Never say that. Instead tell the customer what needs to be done by saying .... ,

' ....

4 'Hang on a second, I'll be right back.' Replace this with .... ,

' ....

5 'No …' ....

B [cassette icon] Listen to Helen Johnson phoning Mr Noor. Are his notes correct?

```
PHONE MESSAGE

FOR:
DATE: ...............................
TIME: ...............................
FROM:  Helen Johnson
OF:  Fleeracker and Co
PHONE:  778 9012

MESSAGE:
Re order EMI 1300 for ABC–10P and ABC-40S. Placed order two weeks
ago and hasn't received ABC–40S yet. Needs it by end of the month.
Phone back.
```

Listen again. What is the reason for delay?

problems in the production department
problems at the supplier's factory
problems with the shipping company

C Practise this dialogue with a partner.

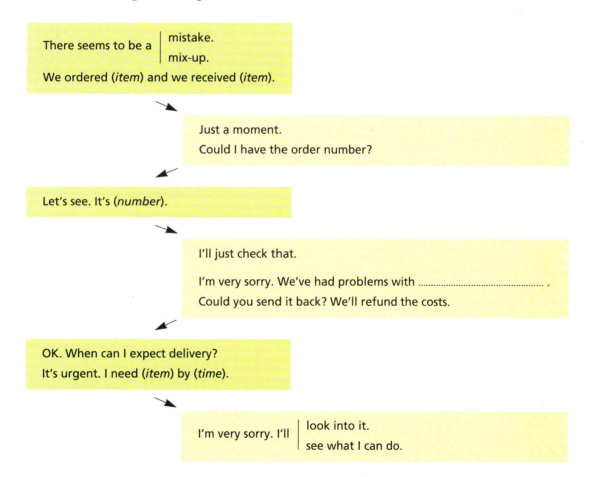

There seems to be a | mistake.
                     | mix-up.
We ordered (*item*) and we received (*item*).

Just a moment.
Could I have the order number?

Let's see. It's (*number*).

I'll just check that.
I'm very sorry. We've had problems with ....
Could you send it back? We'll refund the costs.

OK. When can I expect delivery?
It's urgent. I need (*item*) by (*time*).

I'm very sorry. I'll | look into it.
                      | see what I can do.

D Work in pairs. More problems with deliveries. Student A looks at File 28 on page 121 and Student B looks at File 29 on page 117.

18.3 Finding a solution

A You work in the Sales Department at Pacific Machines. Your boss, Mr Olsen, received this letter from Avalon Industries. What is the problem?

AVALON INDUSTRIES
28 Devonport Road,
Stoke,
Plymouth
PL3 4DW

Mr Olsen
Sales Department
Pacific Machines Ltd
212 Twin Dolphin Drive
Redwood City, CA 94065
USA

29 July 199-

Dear Mr Olsen

I am writing with reference to order no. AS 671 which we received last week.

When we checked the machine we noticed some damage to the case and when we turned it on it did not work. It seems that the machine was not packed properly or tested before dispatch. Please let us know what you intend to do in this matter.

I look forward to hearing from you soon.

Yours sincerely

Brian Rogers

Production Manager

B Mr Olsen puts this note on your desk.

I received this letter this morning. What's strange is that last week we received a fax confirming the arrival of the machine in good condition!

What'll we do?

Bob

What will you do?

refund the money
replace the machine
ask the customer to return the machine so that the company can check it
refuse to accept responsibility

C Write to Mr Rogers telling him what you will do.

You want to refund the money. Look at File 30 on page 119.
You want to replace the machine. Look at File 31 on page 118.
You want to ask the customer to return the machine so that the company can check it.
Look at File 32 on page 120.
You want to refuse to accept responsibility. Look at File 33 on page 122.

19.1 Making predictions

A Match the topics to the symbols on the charts.

food prices   petrol prices   housing costs
wages   unemployment

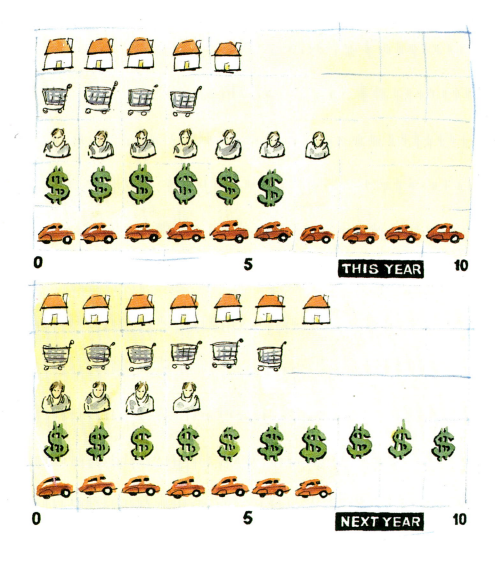

Look at the charts again and make some predictions.

Petrol prices Unemployment Wages Food prices Housing costs	will won't (will not)	increase rise go up decrease fall go down	slightly. slowly. rapidly. dramatically.

B [cassette] Listen and mark the sentence you hear.

1 Petrol prices'll increase in the summer.   [ ]
  Petrol prices increase in the summer.   [ ]

2 We'll import oil from the Middle East.   [ ]
  We import oil from the Middle East.   [ ]

3 Oil'll cost $49 a barrel.   [ ]
  Oil costs $49 a barrel.   [ ]

4 We'll export to the Japanese market.   [ ]
  We export to the Japanese market.   [ ]

5 Exports'll rise in January.   [ ]
  Exports rise in January.   [ ]

6 Imports'll fall in the winter.   [ ]
  Imports fall in the winter.   [ ]

C [cassette] Listen to Mr Green talking about the forecasts in the chart. Write ↑ or ↓.

	↑	↓
Housing costs		
Food		
Unemployment		
Wages		
Petrol prices		

D Work in pairs. You will find some more forecasts. Student A looks at File 34 on page 116 and Student B looks at File 35 on page 119.

19.2 Talking about the future

A Match the topic to the picture.

1 ....   2 ....   3 ....

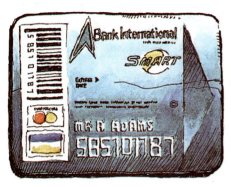

4 ....   5 ....   6 ....

Read this article and put the topics in the correct place.

2000 AND BEYOND

.... (1) will become illegal in the future for all but very small transactions. .... (2) – plastic cards that contain a microprocessor and a memory – will replace cash, credit cards, and most forms of identification in the near future. .... (3) – giant stores that carry a variety of products ranging from food and hardware supplies to clothing and appliances, as well as services such as dry cleaning and haircutting – will grow in number.

.... (4) will be the most important commodity in many industries. By the year 2000, 95% of jobs will be in .... (5) and will require workers who can use computers and other information processing technologies. .... (6) will be the new global workers of the future. Those workers will telecommute over great distances. Companies in the USA, Japan and Europe will compete for these workers in the 21st century.

B Study these examples to show how sure you are something will happen.

I'm certain + will . . .	100%
I expect + will . . .	75%
It's possible + will . . .	50%
I don't think + will . . .	25%
I'm sure + won't . . .	0%

Now listen to people talking about the article. Complete their opinions.

1 .... cash'll become illegal.

2 .... smart cards'll replace credit cards.

3 .... there won't be more hypermarkets.

4 .... information will be the most important commodity.

5 .... so many people'll work in service industries.

6 .... I'll become an electronic immigrant.

Listen again. What reasons do they give for their opinions? What do you think about these forecasts? Compare your opinions with a partner's.

C Look at these topics. Make some predictions about them for the year 2010.

computers	education/training	shopping
robots/automation	living standards	
working hours	the cost of living	the dollar
credit cards	your job	

19.3 Changing the way we work

A Do you have any of these things at home? What do you use them for? Is it work or pleasure?

B Before you read the article on the next page, answer these questions.

1 What percentage of Americans work at home?
2 What do you think the advantages are for:
   a) the company?
   b) the workers?
   c) the environment?

> **Commute:** If you commute, you travel a long distance regularly between your home and your place of work.
>
> **Telecommute:** If you telecommute, you work from home using phone, fax, copier and computer to keep in touch with your company or clients.

Now read the article and check your answers.

THE CHANGING WORKPLACE

Do you hate commuting to work? Perhaps you won't always have to. A study of 521 American corporations says that telecommuting is one of the flexible work arrangements these companies are most likely to consider in the future. At present 26.8 million people – about 20 per cent of the American labor force – work at least part of the time at home.

Computers, fax machines and electronic mail services mean many tasks can be done outside the office – either at home, on the road, or in the field. Telecommuting allows both corporate employees and self-employed contract workers to be more flexible about where they work. Now people can keep in contact with the business world without going to the office every day.

Management can use these flexible workplace arrangements to solve a number of problems in the business world.

* Companies can compete for employees by offering them workplace alternatives.
* Management can hire workers who live too far away to commute.
* Executives can work at home when tasks demand concentration.
* Traveling employees can obtain support from their offices.
* Baby boomers can be with their families and still do overtime by using home offices.
* Corporations can contribute to clean air goals by using telecommuting to help cut down on commuter traffic.

C You will hear three people talking about telecommuting. What do they do? What are their reasons for telecommuting?

D Look at what people say about telecommuting? Do you agree with them?

I can work better at home.
I miss the coffee breaks with my colleagues.
People work better when their boss isn't there.

Revision and consolidation

A **What do you say?** Match the function to the actual words.

1 Make a prediction.	A Be careful!
2 Thank someone.	B We've installed a new machine.
3 Offer to do something.	C Thank you for arranging that.
4 Complain about an order.	D Would you like me to arrange a demonstration?
5 Apologize.	E I'm very sorry. We've had problems with our suppliers.
6 Give news.	F Unemployment will rise steadily over the next five years.
7 Warn someone.	G I'll see what I can do.
8 Promise to do something.	H We haven't received the goods yet.

Work in pairs. Write a short dialogue with some of the phrases above.

B **Vocabulary** Some words mean the same thing, e.g. *phone, call, ring.*
Can you find five pairs in the box?

> book   mistake   consignment   goods   manufacture
> certain   reserve   mix-up   sure   produce

Can you find five pairs of opposites in this box?

> rise   decrease   cheap   supplier   increase
> successful   disappointing   fall   customer
> expensive

C **Reading**

1 Look at these charts. They show products as a percentage of industry's total sales, worldwide. What do you think they describe sales of?

colour televisions
hi-fi
video cassette recorders

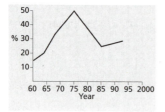

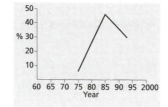

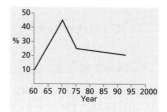

1 ....

2 ....

3 ....

2 Now read this article and find out if you are right.

What Next?

Once every ten years, the consumer-electronics industry – the industry which gives people the means to enjoy live and recorded entertainment in their homes – has come up with a major new product. First, there was colour TV in the 1960s. Next came hi-fi (1970s) and more recently, in the 1980s, the Video cassette recorder (VCR).

When the industry introduced colour TV in the 1960s, it did so just in time. In most big markets, sales of black and white TV had been in decline for several years. Colour TV soon became popular and in the next five years its market share rose from 10% to just over 40%. In the 1970s its share of the market fell dramatically and by the mid 1980s, colour TV accounted for less than 20% of the industry's total sales.

Hi-fi came on the market around the same time as colour television, but its initial share of the market was larger. In 1965 it was already 30% and ten years later it was over 50%. Sales then fell steadily until the mid 1980s and the introduction of the compact disc. Although they were twice as expensive as records, they soon caught on and as a result, hi-fi's market share rose again.

The VCR was the success story of the 1980s. Like television, it was neither a replacement nor an improvement, but a brand new idea. And it created a new demand among consumers. In 1975, the VCR's share of the market was just 5%. Ten years later it was over 40%. Since then, it has declined steadily and is unlikely to rise again.

So the question is what next? What will be the VCR of the next decade?

3 What do you think will happen to these products over the next ten years? Why?

D   Listening

Listen to someone from the consumer electronics industry talking about the future of the industry and complete the graphs on the previous page.

E Speaking Play this game with a partner.

Here is a week's work.

Play with a coin:

Heads – move one square.

Tails – move two squares.

Have conversations with your partner on each square.

START

1 It's Monday morning. What are your plans for this week?

2 A colleague is having problems with the photocopier. What do you say?

You receive an invoic for stationery. It's too high. Phone the supplier and explain.

20 It's Friday morning. A supplier phones to ask why you haven't paid an invoice. Explain and miss a turn.

21 Ask a colleague a question.

22 Your boss wants to know what you have done this week. Name three things or go back to 21.

You haven't finished the monthly report. Miss a turn.

19 It's the end of the evening with your visitor. Thank him for the evening.

18 Your visitor is very interested in the future of your country. Make three predictions.

17 It's Thursday evening. A visitor has invited you out for a meal. Offer to pick him up at the hotel.

16 It's Wednesday night and you work until 10pm. Move forward to 21.

Some paper you ordered has arrived, but it's the wrong size. Phone your supplier.

4 ...ou work until ...o'clock. Move ...orward to 7.

5 You show a visitor around your company. What do you say at the end of the tour?

6 A visitor wants to know if there are any good restaurants in your town. Recommend one.

7 Ask a colleague a question.

8 The fax machine has broken down. Phone the technician and miss a turn.

24 ...'s Friday afternoon. ...our colleague is ...oing home. What do ...ou say?

25 It's Friday evening and you're thinking about your future. Make three predictions.

FINISH

9 Your boss wants to know what you've done today. Name three things (or go back to 7).

10 A visitor wants to know what you can do in your town. Name three things.

14 ...sk a colleague a ...uestion.

13 You forget an appointment with a customer. Phone and apologize. Then miss a turn.

12 You meet an ex-colleague. What news can you give him about your company?

11 You meet an ex-colleague. What news can you give her about your department?

Files

File 15

Find out about the other hotels and decide together which is best for the conference.

	CAPITOL	CROSSROADS	MERIDIAN
ACCOMMODATION			average
SERVICE			excellent
FACILITIES			good
LOCATION			not central
FOOD			good

File 23

You work for Hobson's. Give the caller this information.

```
Easyprint II

Price: £695
Warranty: 6 months
Service contract: £99 per year
Money-back guarantee: 10 days
Delivery: 14 days
```

File 18

You are going to the International Cycle Show in Taipei with two colleagues. Phone the InterCity Hotel in Taipei to book the accommodation. You want 3 single rooms with shower from 19 – 25 April. Find out about the price and ask about restaurants in the hotel.

You can start like this:

This is .... from ....

I'd like to book some accommodation.

File 34

This chart shows figures for this year (T) and forecasts for next year (N). Some forecasts for next year are missing. Find out from your partner what the forecasts for next year are and fill in the chart.

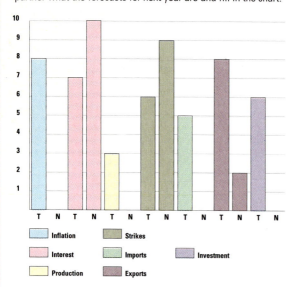

Legend:
- Inflation
- Interest
- Production
- Strikes
- Imports
- Exports
- Investment

You can ask like this:
Will inflation increase next year?
and answer like this:
Yes, it'll increase by ... %.
or *No, it won't. It'll decrease by ...%.*

File 11

You are going on a business trip with a colleague. You are responsible for the **travel arrangements**. These are the travel arrangements.

```
TRAVEL ARRANGEMENTS
October 8
9.45 am      Cathay Pacific flight
             CX 546
6.20 pm      Arrive Rome
             Mr Conti meets us at the airport
             Stay at Sheraton
October 12
8.30 pm      Cathay Pacific flight
             CX 878
October 13
8.05 am      Arrive Hong Kong
```

Find out from your colleague the **business arrangements**. Here are some notes to help you.

October 9: meet who?
October 10: what?
October 11: go where?
October 12: what?
Lunch with Mr Vialli: when?
Visit new factory: when?

What questions can you ask to find out this information?

File 24

You want to invite a new customer to lunch. First write five of these appointments in your diary. You should not have more than one arrangement each day.

Sales Conference (2 days)   Dentist's appointment

Meeting with Sales Director   Visit Head Office

Lunch with sales representative   Day off

Interviews for new sales staff

Quarterly sales meeting

12 Monday	19 Monday
13 Tuesday	20 Tuesday
14 Wednesday	21 Wednesday
15 Thursday	22 Thursday
16 Friday	23 Friday
17 Saturday	24 Saturday
18 Sunday	25 Sunday

Now phone your customer and find a day to meet for lunch

File 17

Read the text about Bob Payton. Your partner will ask you questions about his background.

Bob Payton was born in New York. He studied advertising in Chicago and then joined the advertising agency J. Walter Thompson as assistant marketing manager. He moved to the agency's London office in 1973. Four years later he opened a restaurant in London, The Chicago Pizza Pie Factory. In 1985 he bought a large house in the country and opened a hotel there in 1988. In 1989 he received the 1989 Tourism Personality of the Year award from the English Tourist Board.

Your partner has information about Andrew Robertson. Ask questions so that you can fill in the missing information.

ANDREW ROBERTSON

        Grew up in ....

19.... Came to England.

1978 Studied .... at City of London Polytechnic.

1981 Worked as .... at Oglivy & Mather.

1986 ....

19.... Moved to J. Walter Thompson.

1990 ....

File 6

Read this text and fill in the table. Then find out about your partner's company.

DAF POWER IN PERFORMANCE

DAF is a trend setting company in the commercial vehicle industry and develops and produces engines for commercial vehicles and buses, and other applications.

Turnover of Dfl 5.2 billion.

DAF today is an international business. It has production facilities in the Netherlands, Belgium and the UK, with assembly facilities in eleven other countries. Internationally, it has some 1,000 sales and service points and almost 16,500 employees.

	You	Your partner
Line of business		
Sales		
Number of employees		

File 29

You work for CMA Advertising Gifts, a small mail order company. This is part of your catalogue.

Description	Price
W1/787 Pocket radios	26,95
W1/786 Pocket calculators	2,49

A customer phones you to complain about a delivery. Find out what the problem is. What will you do?

File 1

Dictate these names to your partner.

1 Brown

2 Clark

3 Johnson

4 Pyke

Which one is it?

1 [ ]Green   [ ]Greene

2 [ ]O'Brian   [ ]O'Brien

3 [ ]Reagan   [ ]Regan

4 [ ]Thomson   [ ]Thompson

File 4

Your partner needs some information about these people.

Nilsson AB
OLAF KARLSON
Marketing Director

Rapsgatan 3
Stockholm
Sweden
Tel: 46 8 611 9764
Fax: 46 8 613 7501

Hatchett & Hatchett Ltd
LAURA RATCLIFFE
Accountant

27 London Wall
London
England
Tel: 44 71 374 6310
Fax: 44 71 374 0163

Medica GmbH
ANITA BRINKMANN
Vice President
Molostraße 2
1120 Vienna
Austria
Tel: +43 222 634 144
Fax: +43 222 612 244

DATA DESIGN B.V.
JAN TIMMER
Sales representative
Marconistraat 12
Rotterdam
Holland
Tel: (010) 400711
Fax: (010) 404646

You need some more information about these people. Ask your partner about them.

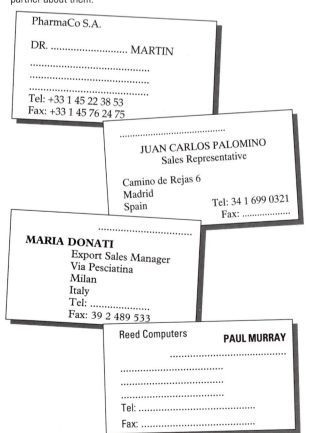

PharmaCo S.A.

DR. .... MARTIN

....
....
....
Tel: +33 1 45 22 38 53
Fax: +33 1 45 76 24 75

....
JUAN CARLOS PALOMINO
Sales Representative

Camino de Rejas 6
Madrid
Spain
Tel: 34 1 699 0321
Fax: ....

....
MARIA DONATI
Export Sales Manager
Via Pesciatina
Milan
Italy
Tel: ....
Fax: 39 2 489 533

Reed Computers   **PAUL MURRAY**
....
....
....
Tel: ....
Fax: ....

File 14

Find out about the other hotels and decide together which is best for the conference.

	CAPITOL	CROSSROADS	MERIDIAN
ACCOMMODATION		excellent	
SERVICE		good	
FACILITIES		OK	
LOCATION		central	
FOOD		not very good	

File 20

You work for Crazy Joe. Give the caller this information.

```
Easyprint II

Price: £549
Warranty: 6 months
Service contract: no
Money-back guarantee: no
Delivery: from stock
```

Now turn to File 22 on page 121.

File 31

Write a letter to Mr Rogers at Avalon Industries and tell him:

he should return the machine to you at Pacific Machines' expense;
you will send a replacement machine as soon as possible.

Start your letter:

Thank you for your letter of 29 July 199- informing us that ...

          YOUR INFORMATION

Finish your letter:

We apologize for the inconvenience and hope that the new consignment will arrive in good condition.

File 9

Ask your partner to:

spell his/her name.
repeat that.
help you write a letter in English.
lend you $5.
phone your boss to say you are ill.

Now think of two more things to ask your partner to do.

File 12

You are going on a business trip with a colleague. You are responsible for the **business arrangements**. These are the arrangements.

```
BUSINESS ARRANGEMENTS
October 9
9.15 am     Meet agent (Ms Spinardi)
1.00 pm     Lunch (Mr Vialli)
3.30 pm     Visit new factory

October 10
9.30 am     Attend production meeting

October 11
All day     Attend fair

October 12 Free day
```

Find out from your colleague the **travel arrangements**. Here are some notes to help you.

Flight: which airline?
Arrive in Rome: when?
Meet us at airport: who?
Hotel: which one?
Leave Rome: when?
Arrive in Hong Kong: when?

What questions can you ask to find out this information?

File 35

This chart shows figures for this year (T) and forecasts for next year (N). Some forecasts for next year are missing. Your partner has this information. Find out what the forecasts for next year are and fill in the chart.

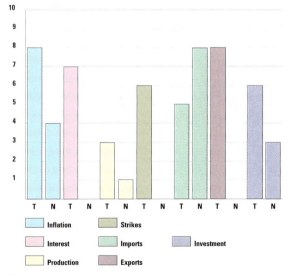

You can ask like this:
Will interest increase next year?

and answer like this:
Yes, it'll increase by .... %.
or *No, it won't. It'll decrease by .... %.*

File 25

Fill in five of these appointments in your diary. You should not have more than one arrangement each day.

Meeting with Purchasing Manager	2 days holiday
Workshop "Time Management"	Visit from supplier
Lunch with new supplier	Doctor's appointment
Visit from Head Office	Trade fair (2 days)

12	Monday	19	Monday
13	Tuesday	20	Tuesday
14	Wednesday	21	Wednesday
15	Thursday	22	Thursday
16	Friday	23	Friday
17	Saturday	24	Saturday
18	Sunday	25	Sunday

A new supplier will phone you to arrange a meeting. When do you have time?

File 30

Write a letter to Mr Rogers at Avalon Industries and tell him:

you will refund the full price of the machine and costs;
he should return the machine to you as soon as possible.

Start like this:
We have received your letter of 29 July 199- in which you told us that ...

YOUR INFORMATION

Finish like this:
Please accept our apologies.

File 8

You are at reception. Ask your partner where these places are:
the Accounts Department
the Personnel Department
the Conference Room

When you find them, mark them on the plan.

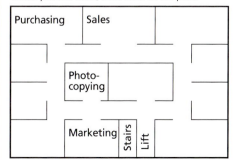

File 7

You are at reception. Ask your partner where these places are:

the Marketing Department
the Purchasing Department
the Photocopying Room

When you find them, mark them on the plan.

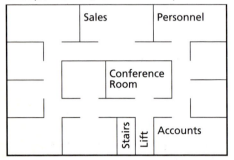

File 32

Write a letter to Mr Rogers at Avalon Industries and tell him:

he should return the machine (at Pacific Machines' cost);
your technician will check the damage;
if the machine was damaged during shipment you will send a replacement. Draw attention to the fax that was sent by Avalon Industries saying that the consignment arrived in good condition.

Start your letter:

We refer to your letter of 29 July 199- in which you informed us of problems with your order no. AS 671.

YOUR INFORMATION

Finish your letter:

While we cannot give you an answer at present, we will look into the matter and write to you as soon as our technicians have checked the machine.

File 13

Find out about the other hotels and decide together which is best for the conference.

	CAPITOL	CROSSROADS	MERIDIAN
ACCOMMODATION	good		
SERVICE	terrible		
FACILITIES	excellent		
LOCATION	central		
FOOD	average		

File 10

Ask your partner to:

tell you the time.
give you his/her telephone number.
meet you on Saturday to help you with your homework.
spell 'personnel'.
lend you his/her credit card.

Now think of two more things to ask your partner to do.

File 19

You work for the InterCity Hotel. Answer the phone and answer the caller's questions. Don't forget to fill in the details on the booking form.

Surname: .... First name(s): ....

Address: ....

Tel: .... Fax: ....

Arrival: .... Departure: ....

Single room(s)	$75
Single room(s) with shower	$100
Double room(s)	$130
Double room(s) with shower	$155

File 5

Read this text and fill in the table. Then find out about your partner's company.

COMPUTER AND COMMUNICATIONS MAKER

Fujitsu is one of the world's top computer and telecommunications makers, with 100,000 employees, annual sales of $18 billion, and projects completed in a hundred countries. A high-tech giant that's a major force in the global information revolution.

FUJITSU

The global computer and communications company.

	You	Your partner
Line of business		
Sales		
Number of employees		

File 28

Some time ago you placed this order with CMA Advertising Gifts.

ORDER NO 03443		
Quantity 50	Description W1/787 Pocket radios	Price 26,95
	Total	1347,50

The delivery arrived this morning. When you unpacked the goods you found 50 pocket calculators. Phone CMA Advertising Gifts and explain.

File 2

Which one is it?

1 [ ] Braun   [ ] Brown
2 [ ] Clark   [ ] Clerk
3 [ ] Johnson   [ ] Johnston
4 [ ] Pike   [ ] Pyke

Dictate these names to your partner.

1 Green
2 O'Brien
3 Regan
4 Thompson

File 26

Your boss is on a business trip. It is now Thursday evening and your boss telephones you to find out what you have done. These are the things you've done.

Monday
  inspect the new factory
  visit Mr Franklin

Tuesday
  meeting with the sales team
  write a report on the meeting

Wednesday
  talk to the export department about new
  delivery conditions

Thursday
  make an appointment with
  Ms Zietsch for next week

Your boss is sure to ask you about the things you haven't done. Think of excuses, e.g. *I haven't had time yet. I've been too busy.*

File 22

You are interested in the Easyprint II Laser Printer. Phone Hobson's and find out the following information.

    Easyprint II

    Price:
    Warranty:
    Service contract:
    Money-back guarantee:
    Delivery:

File 16

Read the text about Andrew Robertson. Your partner will ask you questions about his background.

Andrew Robertson is chief executive of WCRS, the advertising agency. He grew up in Zimbabwe and arrived in England in 1978 to study civil engineering. But after a temporary job on a cold building site in Windsor, he decided to study Economics at City of London Polytechnic instead. His first job in advertising was as trainee media planner with Ogilvy & Mather. By 1986 he was new business director. He moved to J. Walter Thompson in 1989 and in November 1990 he became chief executive of WCRS.

Your partner has information about Bob Payton. Ask questions so that you can fill in the missing information.

BOB PAYTON

1970	Studied advertising in ....
1971	Worked as .... at J. Walter Thompson.
1973	Moved to ....
1977	....
19....	Bought a house in the country.
1988	Opened ....
19....	Received the award *Tourism Personality of the Year*.

File 21

You are interested in the Easyprint II Laser Printer. Phone Crazy Joe and find out the following information.

    Easyprint II

    Price:
    Warranty:
    Service contract:
    Money-back guarantee:
    Delivery:

Now turn to File 23 on page 116.

File 3

You need some information about these people. Ask your partner about them.

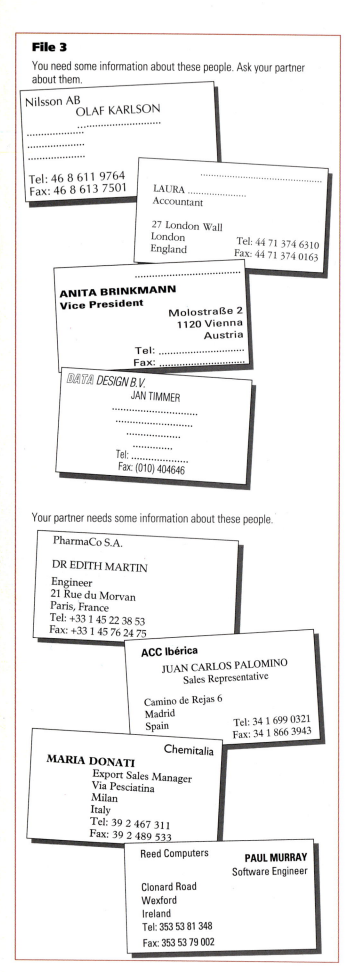

Nilsson AB
OLAF KARLSON
....
....
....
Tel: 46 8 611 9764
Fax: 46 8 613 7501

....
LAURA ....
Accountant

27 London Wall
London
England
Tel: 44 71 374 6310
Fax: 44 71 374 0163

....
ANITA BRINKMANN
Vice President
Molostraße 2
1120 Vienna
Austria
Tel: ....
Fax: ....

DATA DESIGN B.V.
JAN TIMMER
....
....
....
Tel: ....
Fax: (010) 404646

Your partner needs some information about these people.

PharmaCo S.A.

DR EDITH MARTIN
Engineer
21 Rue du Morvan
Paris, France
Tel: +33 1 45 22 38 53
Fax: +33 1 45 76 24 75

ACC Ibérica
JUAN CARLOS PALOMINO
Sales Representative

Camino de Rejas 6
Madrid
Spain
Tel: 34 1 699 0321
Fax: 34 1 866 3943

Chemitalia
MARIA DONATI
Export Sales Manager
Via Pesciatina
Milan
Italy
Tel: 39 2 467 311
Fax: 39 2 489 533

Reed Computers   **PAUL MURRAY**
Software Engineer

Clonard Road
Wexford
Ireland
Tel: 353 53 81 348
Fax: 353 53 79 002

File 33

Write a letter to Mr Rogers at Avalon Industries and tell him:

you refuse to accept responsibility for the damage;
Avalon Industries said the consignment arrived in good condition;
look at the note Mr Olsen wrote on page 104 and use the information in your letter;
Mr Rogers should contact his insurance company and see if they will cover the costs of the damage.

Start your letter:

Thank you for your letter of 29 July 199- informing us of damage to order no. AS 671.

YOUR INFORMATION

Finish your letter:

We are sorry that we cannot help you in this matter.

File 27

You are a department manager. You are away on business. It is Thursday evening. You have asked your assistant to do these things while you're away:

make an appointment with Ms Zietsch for next week

inspect the new factory

send some brochures to Ms Deima

write a report on the meeting

visit Mr Franklin

talk to the export department about new delivery conditions

go to a presentation of the new product

have a meeting with the sales team

Phone your assistant and find out if he or she has done these things yet. If not, ask why: e.g. *Why haven't you … ?*

Tapescripts

1.2 B

1 Recept: Hello, Ms Anopow. How are you?
  Anopow: Not too bad, thanks. And you?
  Recept: Oh fine. How are things in Moscow?
  Anopow: Oh, quite busy at the moment. In fact, we're about to open a new branch in St Petersburg.

2 Braun: Good morning. My name's Braun.
  Recept: Is that Mr Brown from New York or Mr Braun from Frankfurt?
  Braun: Frankfurt.
  Recept: I'm Antonetta Buscotti. Pleased to meet you, Mr Braun.
  Braun: Pleased to meet you too.

3 Santos: Good morning. My name's Santos.
  Recept: From São Paulo?
  Santos: That's right.
  Recept: I'm Antonetta Buscotti. How do you do, Mr Santos?
  Santos: How do you do?
  Recept: Now there's some coffee if you go through to the lounge.

4 Recept: Hello Ms Girardin. It's nice to see you again.
  Girardin: Nice to see you, too.
  Recept: Is Mr Le Grand with you as well?
  Girardin: Er ... no. He's still in Paris.

5 Yin: Hello. I don't think we've met. My name's Yin.
  Pousset: Hi. I'm Jacqueline Pousset. Where are you from, Mr Yin?
  Yin: China. I work in Peking. And you?
  Pousset: I'm from Belgium. Brussels, to be exact.

1.3 A

Woman: Hello Giovanni. Good to see you again. How are things?
Giovanni: Just fine, fine. And you?
Woman: Oh, not too bad. Giovanni, do you know Bryan Turner, our new Personnel Manager? Bryan, this is Giovanni Toncini. He's from Italy. He works in Milan.
Bryan: Pleased to meet you, Mr Toncini.
Giovanni: Please, call me Giovanni.
Bryan: And I'm Bryan.
Woman: Have a seat, Giovanni.
Giovanni: Thank you.
Woman: How about some coffee? Giovanni?
Giovanni: Yes, please. Cream and sugar, please.

2.1 A

Lampl: I don't think we've met. I'm Richard Lampl.
Braun: Nice to meet you. My name's Braun, George Braun.
Lampl: Pleased to meet you, Mr Braun.
Braun: Please call me George.
Lampl: And I'm Richard. What do you do, George?
Braun: I'm in computers. I'm a software engineer.
Lampl: Really. Who do you work for?
Braun: I'm with ABC Software.
Lampl: Ah ... I need someone who can advise us about installing computers.
Braun: Well, give me a call some time. Look, here's my card.
Lampl: Thank you. I'll do that.

2.1 D

The majority of the people in Singapore work in manufacturing, commerce and the service sectors. A total of 11·5% of the workforce are professional or technical workers; by that I mean people like accountants, engineers and lawyers. A further 7% are employed in administrative jobs. These are executives and managers, supervisors and so on. 15·5% of the workforce have clerical or office jobs. That's not only office clerks, but also secretaries, typists and receptionists. Just over a third of all jobs are in production, 36% to be exact. The remaining 30% work in other fields, such as sales.

2.2 A

Recept: ABC Software.
Lampl: This is Richard Lampl from Morgan Enterprises. I'd like to speak to Mr Braun.
Recept: Is that Robert Brown or George Braun?
Lampl: Er ... George Braun.
Recept: Hold the line, please.
Lampl: Thank you.

Brown: Brown.
Lampl: This is Richard Lampl from Morgan Enterprises. Is that Mr George Braun?
Brown: Sorry, what's your name?
Lampl: Lampl. L.A.M.P.L.
Brown: I'm sorry, Mr Lampl. This is Robert Brown. I think you've got the wrong extension.
Lampl: Oh, could you put me through to Mr George Braun, please?
Brown: Just a moment.

Braun: Braun.
Lampl: Is that Mr Braun? Mr George Braun?
Braun: Speaking.
Lampl: Oh, at last. My name's Lampl. We met a couple of ...
Braun: Sorry, who's speaking?
Lampl: Richard Lampl. L.A.M.P.L. From Morgan Enterprises. We met at a party ...

2.3 B

1 Walker: Walker speaking.
  Martin: Is that you, Barbara? It's Julian Martin.
  Walker: Oh, hi Julian. How can I help?
  Martin: Can you give me some information about Maria? You know, the accountant at APG.
  Walker: Sure. What do you want to know?
  Martin: What's her surname?
  Walker: Oliveira.
  Martin: Sorry, can you spell that?
  Walker: Yes, O.L.I.V.E.I.R.A.
  Martin: What's her address?
  Walker: Rua Cachambi. That's C.A.C.H.A.M.B.I.
  Martin: C.A.C.H.A.M.B.I.
  Walker: Right. Rua Cachambi 2. Rio de Janeiro, Brazil.
  Martin: Rio de Janeiro, Brazil. OK. Now, what's her fax number?
  Walker: 55 21 394 6845.
  Martin: I'm sorry, can you repeat that?
  Walker: Sure. 55 21 394 6845.
  Martin: Right, thanks very much.
  Walker: You're welcome. See you at the meeting on Friday. Bye.
  Martin: Bye.

2 Recept: Sand & Sand.
  Spencer: This is Tamara Spencer. Can I speak to Tom Morrison, please?
  Recept: Hold the line, please.

  Morrison: Morrison speaking.
  Spencer: Hello. It's Tamara Spencer.
  Morrison: Oh, hello Tamara. What can I do for you?
  Spencer: Well, I need some information about Yoshi Takahashi.
  Morrison: Sure. What do you want to know?
  Spencer: Who does he work for?
  Morrison: Oceania.
  Spencer: How do you spell that?
  Morrison: O.C.E.A.N.I.A.
  Spencer: O.C.E.A.N.I.A. Right. What does he do?
  Morrison: He's a sales representative.
  Spencer: Ah. What's his telephone number?
  Morrison: Just a minute. 813 3827 4848.
  Spencer: Sorry, can you say that again?
  Morrison: It's 813 3827 4848. Anything else?
  Spencer: No, that's everything, thanks.
  Morrison: You're welcome. Bye for now.
  Spencer: Bye.

3.1 C

1 Inter: Who do you work for?

Man: Goldstar Electric. It's a Korean company. It's part of the Lucky-Goldstar Group.

Inter: Oh. And where do you work?

Man: At the headquarters. That's in Seoul. But I travel a lot. We have branches in over 120 countries, so I'm not actually in my office that often.

2 Inter: Can you tell me something about your company?

Woman: We're in the financial services business. Traveller's checks, charge cards, banking and that kind of thing. I'm sure you've heard of us … American Express. The head office is in New York but we have offices all over the world.

3 Inter: Who do you work for?

Man: Alcatel.

Inter: That's a Dutch company, isn't it?

Man: Yes, that's right. The headquarters are in Amsterdam, but I don't work there. I work in Rotterdam. We operate in 120 countries and manufacture in 22.

4.1 A

1 Woman: Oh, good morning. I've got an appointment with Miss Vetta in the Personnel Department.

Recept: Ah, good morning. You must be Mrs Peters.

Woman: Yes, that's right.

Recept: Miss Vetta asked me to send you up when you arrive. Personnel is on the first floor.

Woman: The first floor.

Recept: Yes, that's right.

Woman: Thank you.

2 Man: Good afternoon. I've got a delivery for the marketing department.

Recept: Oh, that looks heavy. Marketing is on the third floor. You can take the elevator, if you like.

3 Woman: Excuse me, can you tell me how to get to Mr Chang's office in the after-sales department?

Recept: Well, after-sales is on the second floor, but I think Mr Chang is on holiday this week.

4.1 B

1 Man 1:   Excuse me, where's Mr Lee's office?

Man 2:   Mr Lee's office? Take the elevator up to the fourth floor. When you come out of the elevator, go right. Then left at the end of the corridor.

Man 1:   Right and then left.

Man 2:   Yes. It's the first office on the right.

Man 1:   First office on the right. Ah, next to Miss Ho's office.

Man 2:   Yes, that's right.

2 Woman: Excuse me, I'm looking for the Purchasing Manager's office.

Man: Oh, you mean Ms Wong.

Woman: Er…yes.

Man: Well, go up to the fourth floor. When you come out of the elevator, go left. It's the second door on the left. At the end of the corridor.

3 Woman: Excuse me, I'm looking for Mr Tan.

Man: Is that Mr Tan in Marketing?

Woman: Er…yes, I think so.

Man: Oh, his office isn't on this floor. It's on the fourth floor. Go down the stairs and turn left. At the end of the corridor go right.

Woman: Left, then right.

Man: It's the first door on the left. Opposite the conference room. Look, I've got to go down there. I'll show you where it is.

4.2 D

1 A lot of my work is routine secretarial work. You know, answering the phone, writing letters, that kind of thing. Customers often want information about our products, so I have to write a lot of letters. Another part of my job is to organize seminars. I organize speakers, I invite the guests, arrange a venue and even accomodation.

2 I have a lot of contact with customers because they phone us when they have problems with our machines. Which is quite often. They phone us because they need spare parts - something's broken or worn out - and then I take the orders and send parts to the customers.

3 I'm responsible for hiring and firing! When there's a vacancy, I write the job description. Then I advertise the position. Either in the company or in a newspaper. And I interview the applicants and select them. And finally I draw up their contract.

4.3 A

Recept: International. Good morning.

Baffini: Good morning. This is Mr Biondi of Viva Agency. Could you put me through to Mr Suzuki, please?

Recept: I'm afraid he's not in today. Can I take a message?

Baffini: Yes please. Can you ask him to call me back?

Recept: Of course. Who's calling please?

Baffini: My name's Biondi and my number …

Recept: Oh, can you spell that, please?

Baffini: Yes, that's B.I.O.N.D.I.

Recept: B.I.O.N.D.I.

Baffini: And my number is 39-3-67 78 80 12

Recept: 39-3-67 78 80 12. Right, Mr Biondi. I'll ask Mr Suzuki to call you back.

Baffini: Thank you very much.

Recept: You're welcome.

5 D

Presenter: And now continuing our series of interviews with people in local industry, we have an interview with Geoff Story, the Managing Director of Donaldson Packaging.

Presenter: Mr Story, you're the Managing Director of Donaldson Packaging.

Story: That's right.

Presenter: Could you tell us something about your company?

Story: Well, Donaldson Packaging is part of the PSSI Packaging group. PSSI, as you probably know, is a Swedish company. Donaldson Packaging itself is really two companies. Donaldson Packaging Ltd manufactures board for packaging. Most of it is for the food industry, although we also produce packaging material for other goods too. We have two factories, one here in Stalybridge and a second one just outside Bristol. And Donaldson Wellpack Ltd, that's the other company, markets our packaging systems and machines. Most of them are for the British market, although we do export as well.

Presenter: And where are the UK headquarters?

Story: Here in Stalybridge.

Presenter: I see. And how many employees does Donaldson Packaging have.

Story: Almost 600. 598 to be exact.

Presenter: Thank you very much for talking to us, Mr Story. And now back to the studio.

6.3 B

1 Inter: What do you do, Ros?

Ross: I'm a lawyer.

Inter: Do you like your job?

Ross: Yes, I do. The work's very interesting, I get on really well with my colleagues and the salary's great.

Inter: Are there any bad things?

Ross: Well, I work very long hours … ten hours a day is quite normal. And if something important comes up I'm often in the office until eight or nine in the evening. Or I take work home. The other bad thing is that I don't have much holiday – only 20 days a year. Actually, I'd prefer less money and more holiday.

2 Inter: Tell me something about your job, Jan.

Jan: Well, I'm a shift supervisor.

Inter: So you work shifts?

Jan: That's right, yes. One week I work from 6 in the morning to 2 in the afternoon, the next week from 2 in the afternoon to 10 in the evening and the third week from 10 in the evening until 6 in the morning.

Inter:	That must be terrible!
Jan:	Actually, I quite like it. I don't mind getting up early and I love finishing at two in the afternoon And I get a lot of time off between shifts. I also get a lot of holiday. Six weeks a year.
Inter:	That sounds wonderful! But is there anything you don't like about your job?
Jan:	Well, the pay's not too good.

3	Inter:	Ute, what do you do?
	Ute:	I'm a secretary. I work in R&D.
	Inter:	And do you like your job?
	Ute:	Yes, I do. You see, I don't just sit at my desk and write reports. I have a lot of contact with our clients, and I enjoy that. And I have a terrific boss.
	Inter:	Is there anything you don't like about your job?
	Ute:	Well, the journey's terrible. It takes me an hour to get to work. And then we have flexitime. But it's not very flexible because I'm always in minus at the end of the month. So I have to stay in the office even if there's no work. I'd prefer to work when there's something to do and go home when there isn't.

7.1 D

1	Stuart:	Sam Stuart speaking.
	Taylor:	This is Juliet Taylor from Personnel Potential Inc, Meriden. Could I speak to Thomas Schwartz, please.
	Stuart:	I'm afraid he's on vacation this week.
	Taylor:	I see. Well, perhaps you can help me. We've had a lot of enquiries about your executive secretary courses, but we haven't got any brochures. Could you send us some … about fifty.
	Stuart:	Sure, no problem.
	Taylor:	Have you got our address? It's 114 Canal Street …
	Stuart:	Sorry, 140 or 114?
	Taylor:	114. One one four.
	Stuart:	Right, 114 Canal Street.
	Taylor:	Meriden. That's M.E.R.I.D.E.N.
	Stuart:	M.E.R.I.D.E.N.
	Taylor:	Connecticut 06450.
	Stuart:	06450. Right. I'll mail them to you, Ms Taylor.
	Taylor:	Thanks very much. And … er … give my regards to Tom when you see him.

2	Cameron:	MacPherson and Company. Cameron speaking.
	Jansson:	This is Erica Jansson from Nordgren, Sweden.
	Cameron:	Hello, Ms Jansson. What can I do for you?
	Jansson:	I'm phoning about Mr Axelsson's visit to Glasgow in July. Could you book a hotel for him?
	Cameron:	Yes, of course. At the Crown or the King's Head?
	Jansson:	Er … The Crown. A single room with bath. From the twenty-first to the twenty-third of July.
	Cameron:	Right. Single room with bath for the twenty-first to the twenty-third of July.
	Jansson:	That's right.
	Cameron:	Right. I'll see to it, Ms Jansson and send you a confirmation of the reservation.
	Jansson:	Thank you very much.
	Cameron:	You're welcome. Bye.
	Jansson:	Goodbye.

3	Operator:	Miles and Cross. Good morning.
	Takamit:	Is that the Sales Department?
	Operator:	Hold the line, please. I'll put you through.
	Sales:	Sales Department.
	Takamit:	This is Mr Takamitsu from Yokohama. We've got a bit of a problem with parts in Production at the moment. Could you send us a batch of f110s by the end of the week?
	Sales:	How many do you need?
	Takamit:	500 pieces.
	Sales:	500 pieces? By the end of the week? Well, I'll see what I can do. But send me a confirmation this time to make it official.
	Takamit:	Could you send them straight to the factory? It's urgent.

7.2 D

Well, I usually get to the office by about nine. I always mean to get there earlier, but I never quite manage it. On a normal day, I work until about five. But if we have an important meeting – and that's once or twice a month – I work later, until seven or eight at night.

I get 30 days holiday a year, so I'm very lucky. I usually try to take a long holiday in the summer, you know, three or four weeks. Then I like to travel, to go away and see something different. And I always take a week in February. I go skiing then.

Unfortunately, I don't have time to exercise during the week, although if the weather's nice I go for a walk at lunchtime. But I cycle or play tennis most weekends. And in the winter I go skiing.

I think I'm organized. You have to be in my job.

I go to an Italian course once a week after work. The other evenings I meet friends. We go to the cinema, or to a bar or restaurant.

Well, I don't smoke, but I do drink a lot of coffee. I think I'm a very calm person. I don't worry and I don't get angry very easily. Do I ever think of changing my job? Well, I don't think I'll stay here for ever, but I'm quite happy at the moment.

8.1 B

Colleague:	When are you off then?
Alicia:	I'm leaving on Sunday night.
Colleague:	What's your schedule?
Alicia:	I arrive in Singapore on Monday. The plane lands at 5.30 in the afternoon and Mr Wong's meeting me at the airport. Tuesday's a busy day. I'm attending the conference in the morning and in the afternoon I'm meeting Mr Goh.
Colleague:	Who's he?
Alicia:	One of the new agents.
Colleague:	Oh. Are you seeing Mr Hu?
Alicia:	Yes, I'm seeing him on Wednesday. We're inspecting the factory in the morning and I'm having dinner with him in the evening.
Colleague:	You've got a full schedule!
Alicia:	Oh, that's not everything. I'm free on Thursday, but I'm going to the fair on Friday and then on Saturday I'm catching the 12 o'clock plane to Sydney.
Colleague:	What are you doing in Sydney?

8.2 C

First try

Operator:	FabriCo.
Singh:	This is Mr Singh from SolarTec. I'd like to speak to Mr Paton.
Operator:	Sorry, who's calling?
Singh:	My name's Singh. S.I.N.G.H.
Operator:	Hold the line, Mr Singh. I'll put you through to Mr Paton. … I'm afraid his line's engaged.
Singh:	Oh. I'll try again later.
Operator:	Have you got his extension number?
Singh:	No, I don't think I have.
Operator:	It's 213.
Singh:	Thank you very much. Goodbye.

Second try

Paton:	Paton speaking.
Singh:	Hello Mr Paton. This is Mr Singh from SolarTec.
Paton:	Oh hello, Mr Singh.
Singh:	I'd like to arrange a meeting some time next week.
Paton:	Yeah, OK. When?
Singh:	Are you free on Tuesday?
Paton:	I'm afraid I'm seeing our auditor in the morning.
Singh:	Well, what about the afternoon?
Paton:	Yeah, that's fine.
Singh:	Is 2 o'clock all right?
Paton:	Yeah, yeah, that's fine.
Singh:	Well, see you on Tuesday at two o'clock.

8.3 C

Dombradi: Dombradi speaking.
Shaw: Is that you Gabor? This is Frank Shaw.
Dombradi: Oh hello, Frank. Nice to hear you.
Shaw: Listen. I'm coming to Budapest in October and I'd like to call in to discuss the marketing of the XJ 3.
Dombradi: Great. When are you planning to come?
Shaw: Well, either the fourteenth or the sixteenth. What suits you best?
Dombradi: Let me check my diary. Right. Here we are. Er … I'm afraid I can't make the fourteenth. I've got to see a customer then. But I'm free on the sixteenth.
Shaw: Right. Wednesday the sixteenth. Morning or afternoon?
Dombradi: The morning's better.
Shaw: OK. Shall we say nine o'clock?
Dombradi: Can we make it half past nine?
Shaw: Oh, yes. That's fine by me. I'll just make a note of that. Well, nice talking to you, Gabor. And I'll see you on the sixteenth at nine thirty.

9.1 B

Rufer: Hello, Mr Harris.
Harris: Hello.
Rufer: Nice to see you again! How are you?
Harris: Oh, not too bad, thanks.
Rufer: And did you arrive this morning?
Harris: Yes, by train from Brussels.
Rufer: Did you have a good journey?
Harris: No, not really. The train was late and it was very crowded.
Rufer: Oh, I'm sorry to hear that. Were you in Brussels on business?
Harris: Yes, I was at a conference. Unfortunately, I didn't have time to look round the city. Next time, perhaps.
Rufer: Yes, Brussels is a very nice city. Now, can I get you anything? A cup of coffee?
Harris: Yes, thank you. That would be nice.

9.2 D

1 Man: So what was it like?
Sarah: Great! I really enjoyed it. Some of the talks were very good and there was an excellent atmosphere. It was a pity it was so short. There simply wasn't enough time to talk to everyone.
Man: Did you see Henri Bertillon?
Sarah: Yes, we had lunch together on the last day. He sends his regards and hopes to see you there next time.
Man: Thanks. So it was a good week?
Sarah: Yes, the only problem was that my hotel was a bit far out though.
Man: Oh dear. Where did you stay?

2 Man: Hello, Isobel. How was your day?
Isobel: Tiring! There was a lot of interest in our products and our stand was really crowded.
Man: So it was successful?
Isobel: Oh, yes. And I think we made a lot of good contacts.
Man: Really, you must be glad you came.
Isobel: Oh, yes. Definitely.
Man: Was your boss pleased?
Isobel: He wasn't there!
Man: He wasn't there? Where was he?
Isobel: He was on holiday.

3 Man : Hello, I see you're back. How was it?
Pedro: Well, it was nice to be out of the office for a few days. And the hotel was fantastic. Swimming pool, sauna, everything. And terrific food.
Man : Did you actually learn anything?
Pedro: Yes, I think so.
Man : So you speak fluent English now?
Pedro: Well, not quite. But I learnt a lot. In fact, I think I'll go again next year.

9.3 B

Harada: Is that Mr Sarasin? This is Yoshi Harada from Osaka Industries.
Sarasin: Hello, Mr Harada. How are you?
Harada: Fine, thanks. And yourself?
Sarasin: I can't complain.
Harada: Look, I'm coming to Bangkok next month and I'd like to know if you can recommend a hotel.
Sarasin: Well, Mr Harada, Bangkok has a lot of excellent hotels.
Harada: The travel agent recommended three hotels – the Ambassador, The Royal Orchid Sheraton and the Regent.
Sarasin: Well, it depends what's important for you. All three have excellent business facilities. The Regent's in a very quiet area and still quite close to the business centre. It has very good sporting facilities, tennis and so on. The Ambassador's near the river. But it's fairly difficult to get a room because they often hold large conferences there. The restaurants have an excellent reputation. The Sheraton's good for relaxing. They can arrange leisure events and so on. They have a service where you can hire one of the hotel's translators if you need one.
Harada: Which one would you stay in?
Sarasin: I think I'd choose the Regent. Because of the location and the surroundings.
Harada: I think I'll follow your advice. Thanks for your help.
Sarasin: My pleasure. And give me a call when you're in Bangkok.

10 D

Boss: Now Andrew, what's happening next month?
Andrew: Well, I'm spending the first week at ReadyMix. I'll be there from the fourth to the sixth. I'm coming back here for the Thursday so I can start preparing for the Paris conference the following week.
Boss: Ah yes. Now when is that?
Andrew: From the fourteenth to the sixteenth. I'm flying out on the Wednesday night and coming back on the Sunday. My wife's coming with me and we'll spend the weekend there.
Boss: Good idea. Why not? I always like going to Paris myself. Now when are you seeing Mr Ashdown?
Andrew: Before I go to Paris. On the twelfth. I'm presenting the findings then.
Boss: Good. Right. Now there's a meeting with AutoTec on the eighteenth. Can you come to that?
Andrew: On the eighteenth. Just a minute. Yes, that'll be fine. I'll just make a note of that.
Boss: What else are you doing that week?
Andrew: I'm going to ReadyMix on the Wednesday and Thursday.
Boss: Good. And are you taking a long weekend?
Andrew : Yes, I am. What with the public holiday on the Monday. I'm going away with the family.
Boss: Ah, that's nice.
Andrew: And the rest of the week is free at the moment, but I'm sure it won't stay that way.

11.1 C

Inter: Can you tell me something about yourself, Jiro?
Jiro: Well, I left school when I was eighteen. That was in 1983. And then I went to university. I studied Politics.
Inter: And that was in Toyko?
Jiro: Yes, that's right. I was at Toyko University for four years. I finished my course in 1987.
Inter: And what did you do after that?
Jiro: I got a job with C. Itoh. You know, the trading company. I joined the Sales department as a trainee sales manager.
Inter: And did you enjoy it?
Jiro: Yes, I did.
Inter: How long did you stay there?
Jiro: For three years. And then I went to England. You see, the company sent me to London. They wanted me to learn English. So I spent two years in England, learning English. I also took a course in German while I was there.

Inter:	So you speak German.
Jiro:	Jawohl!
Inter:	What did you do after that?
Jiro:	I came back to Japan in June 1992 and I went back to my old department as assistant sales manager. And that's where I work now.
Inter:	Right. Can you tell me something about your present job?
Jiro:	Yes, well, I'm responsible for …

11.3 B

1 Inter:	Veronique, what was your first job?
Veron:	Well, when I left school I trained as a clerk in a pharmaceutical company. That lasted for two years. My first job was as a secretary to one of the doctors.
Inter:	And what were your duties?
Veron:	I wrote reports. Well, I mean, my boss dictated them to me, and I typed them.
Inter:	Did you enjoy it?
Veron:	Well, the people were nice. I liked the people I worked with. But I didn't really like the job itself. It was boring. All that dictation. The only good thing was that I learnt a lot of English. All the reports were in English!
Inter:	And how long did you stay there?
Veron:	Oh, only about six months. Then there was a vacancy in the personnel department. So I applied for a job there. That's where I work now.
Inter:	And do you prefer that?
Veron:	Oh yes. The work is much more interesting. But I don't have so much opportunity to use my English.

2 Inter:	Can you tell me something about your first job?
Daniela:	Well, yes. It was with a large international company. They have a trainee programme for people from university and, well, that was my first job, trainee marketing manager.
Inter:	What exactly did you do?
Daniela:	Well, the programme lasted eighteen months. During that time I worked in different departments – in personnel, purchasing, marketing and such things. I also went out with the sales representatives to visit customers.
Inter:	Did you enjoy it?
Daniela:	Yes, I did. I didn't really know what I wanted to do when I left university, so it was good to see what the different departments did. It was really practical.
Inter:	It sounds interesting.
Daniela:	Yes, it was. But it was very badly paid. I did the same work as other people. I think a lot of the trainees feel they are a cheap source of labour.
Inter:	Would you do it again?
Daniela:	Sure. I learnt a lot. And found out where I really wanted to work.

12.1 B

Clerk:	Carlton Hotel. Can I help you?
Gordon:	Good morning. This is Wendy Gordon calling from Cycles Unlimited in Manchester. I'd like to book some accommodation for the International Cycle Show.
Clerk:	What exactly do you need?
Gordon:	Three single rooms with shower. From the nineteenth to the twenty-fifth of April.
Clerk:	Just a minute. I'll check that. I'm very sorry, but we haven't got any single rooms for the night of the nineteenth. We're fully booked up because of the fair.
Gordon:	Oh dear.
Clerk:	There are probably some rooms at the InterCity Hotel. Have you got their phone number?
Gordon:	Er, no I haven't. Could you give it to me?
Clerk:	Sure. It's 382 4738.
Gordon:	382 4738. OK. I'll try them. And thanks very much for your help.

12.2 C

Man 1:	Good morning. Can I help you?
Man 2:	Yes, I'm interested in your range of mountain bikes for children.
Man 1:	Right. Well, we've got a new model here. If you come over here, this way. It's this one.
Man 2:	Could you tell me something about it?
Man 1:	Well, it's suitable for children from the age of ten upwards. We have a boy's model and a girl's model. The boy's model's available in yellow and purple. The girl's model … that's this one here … is available in grey and pink. You know, it's only been on the market for a few months, but it's very popular.
Man 2:	Mmm. What does it cost?
Man 1:	The recommended retail price is $159.
Man 2:	$159. For both models?
Man 1:	That's right, yes. For the boy's and the girl's model.
Man 2:	Right. And what about delivery time?
Man 1:	We can deliver from stock.
Man 2:	I see. Now, what about discount? Can you give me a good discount on a large order?
Man 1:	Well, it depends on the size of the order. I'll have to check that. Perhaps you could give me your name and address?
Man 2:	Here's my card.
Man 1:	Thank you. Look, would you like a copy of our brochure in the meantime.

12.3 B

Operator:	Del Mar Sporting.
Hirst:	My name's Colin Hirst from Waters Sportswear, Australia. Could I speak to Mr Sung in Sales, please?
Operator:	Hold the line, Mr Hirst. I'll put you through.
Sung:	Sung speaking.
Hirst:	This is Colin Hirst from Waters Sportswear, Australia. We met at the Sporting Goods Show in Taipei last April.
Sung:	Ah yes, I remember. What can I do for you, Mr Hirst?
Hirst:	I'd like to place an order for some rucksacks, daypacks and travel bags.
Sung:	I see. I'll just note down the details. What exactly do you want?
Hirst:	100 rucksacks. That's catalog number RS 101.
Sung:	100 of RS 101.
Hirst:	And then in the same line, 100 daypacks. That's catalog number DP 101. And 100 travel bags. Catalog number TB 51.
Sung:	100 of DP 101 and 100 TB 51. Right.
Hirst:	That's right. Can I just confirm the prices? The rucksacks are $399 each, the daypacks are $99 and the travel bags are $199.
Sung:	That's right.
Hirst:	Now you said you could let me have a discount on a large order. I think you said 10%.
Sung:	Yes, that'll be all right. That makes $62,730.
Hirst:	Yes, that's fine. By the way, as it's a first order we'll be paying by letter of credit.
Sung:	That's fine.
Hirst:	Just one last question. When can we expect delivery?
Sung:	Erm, in about four weeks?
Hirst:	Fine. I'll put our order in the post.

13.2 A

Come to Computerworld this weekend. We're having our biggest sale ever! Yes, we are selling stock from the widest range of computers at the lowest prices! Even the most modern computers are at low, low prices. Come and see the largest selection of computers and the cheapest prices in town. Don't forget, for the best service come to Computerworld.

13.2 C

Off Sup:	Office Supply. Good morning. Can I help you?
Caller:	Good morning. Yes, I'd like some information about the *Easyprint II*.
Off Sup:	Uh uh. What exactly would you like to know?
Caller:	Well, first of all, how much does it cost?
Off Sup:	Can you hold on a minute. I'll go and check that. Hello, we offer it for £699.
Caller:	699. I see. And what sort of warranty do you offer on that? Is it a one-year warranty?
Off Sup:	Yes, it is. 12 months from the date of purchase.

Caller:	Good. And could you tell me something about service? Do you offer on-site service?
Off Sup:	Yes, we do. It's free for the length of the warranty. And then £120 a year after that.
Caller:	Right. And what about other guarantees?
Off Sup:	Well, there's a 14-day money-back guarantee if you're not satisfied with the printer. Or if you have any problems, just bring it in and you can have a refund.
Caller:	Fine. And what about delivery? How soon can you deliver it to my office?
Off Sup:	Well, we usually have the *Easyprint* in stock, but I'm afraid there's a slight delay on orders at the moment. We could let you have it at the end of the month.
Caller:	Oh. It's the second today. That means another four weeks.

14.2 A

First version:

1 Ernst:	Ernst.
Grimes:	Hello. Mr Ernst?
Ernst:	Yes, speaking.
Grimes:	This is Christine Grimes. I want you to have lunch with me at the Atlas restaurant next week. I want to discuss our new product with you.
Ernst:	When?
Grimes:	Are you free on Tuesday?
Ernst:	No, I'm not. I'm busy. I haven't got time.
Grimes:	Well, Thursday then.
Ernst:	Yeah, that's OK. What time?
Grimes:	12.30.
Ernst:	OK. See you at the Atlas on Thursday at 12.30.

Second version:

2 Ernst:	Good morning.
Grimes:	Hello. This is Christine Grimes. I'd like to speak to Mr Ernst.
Ernst:	Speaking. How are you, Mrs Grimes?
Grimes:	Fine, fine. Look, I'd like to discuss our new product with you. Would you like to have lunch at the Atlas some time next week?
Ernst:	That sounds nice. When exactly?
Grimes:	Well, how about Tuesday?
Ernst:	That's very kind of you, but I'm afraid I can't make Tuesday. I've got to go to Head Office.
Grimes:	That's a pity. Does Thursday suit you?
Ernst:	Yeah, that would be fine. What time?
Grimes:	Shall we say 12.30.
Ernst:	Yeah, that's fine. Next Thursday at 12.30 at the Atlas. I'll look forward to it.

14.3 B

1 Woman 1:	Would you like a starter?
Woman 2:	Yes, that would be nice. Can you help me with the menu?
Woman 1:	Yes, of course. Now these are soups here.
Woman 2:	Ah yes. This one's tomato soup. But what's this – Schneckensuppe?
Woman 1:	That's a local speciality. Snails. It's very popular here. Would you like to try it?
Woman 2:	Hmm. I don't think so!
2 Woman:	What would you like for your main course?
Man:	What can you recommend?
Woman:	Well, the caldeirada is usually very good here.
Man:	Caldeirada. That's fish, isn't it?
Woman:	Yes, that's right. It's a kind of stew, fish stew. With lots of different fish.
Man:	Mm, fish. Yes, that sounds nice. I think I'll have that.
3 Man 1:	What's this – bagare baingan?
Man 2:	It's a kind of vegetable. I think it's aubergine in English.
Man 1:	Aubergine?
Man 2:	Oh, in the States you call it egg plant, don't you?
Man 1:	Oh, egg plant. Mm. Is it hot?
Man 2:	Not really. It's quite mild. But it's very rich.

4 Man:	How about a dessert? I'm going to have phal mava.
Wom:	Oh, what's that?
Man:	It's a fruit salad with melon, bananas, oranges, grapes and mango.
Wom:	Mm. It sounds very refreshing.
Man:	Would you like to try it? Or something else?
Wom:	Er … I think I'll just have a coffee.

15 D

Inter:	You've just bought a SuperDesk organizer. Can I ask you a few questions about your purchase?
Customer:	Sure.
Inter:	Is this organizer for yourself or is it a gift for someone else?
Customer:	It's for myself.
Inter:	Right. What are you going to use it for?
Customer:	Well, mainly for work. You know, customers' addresses and phone numbers, appointments, meetings, projects, that kind of thing.
Inter:	I see. And why did you choose a SuperDesk organizer?
Customer:	Well, I saw an advertisement for them in a magazine. And the price. They're much cheaper than other organizers. Very reasonable, really.
Inter:	OK. Now, why did you choose this particular one?
Customer:	Well, I did have an organizer before, but it was too small. I couldn't keep my papers in it. And to be honest, I liked the colour.
Inter:	Fine. Now can I ask you a couple of questions about yourself? What do you do?
Customer:	I'm a Product Manager.
Inter:	Right. And can you tell me what you do in your free time? Have a look at this list.
Customer:	Well, I play tennis. I enjoy eating out and going to the theatre. What else is there? Foreign travel … no, I don't usually go abroad for holidays. And I'm interested in current affairs. That's all.
Inter:	Right. Now, if I could just note down your personal details. Are you married?

16.1 B

1 Bianchi:	My name's Mario Bianchi. I've got an appointment with Mr Spackmann.
Porter:	Right. I'll just let him know you're here. … Is that Mr Spackmann? Mr Bianchi is here. … He'll be down in a minute. Now you need this for security. And could you sign the visitor's book please? Er, here.
Bianchi:	Yes, of course.
2 Man:	The new machine is very similar to the old one, although it is a lot faster. The line runs at 140 packs a minute, although it can do up to 190 packs.
Bianchi:	That sounds very impressive.
Man:	I'm afraid you'll have to wear an overall. It's a hygiene requirement. It's also very important not to touch the machinery. Please come this way.
3 Man:	Right. Here we are. Now this is where the machine sorts and inspects the tablets. Please don't touch them!
Bianchi:	Oh, I'm sorry.
Man:	And over here it counts them and puts them into bottles. The bottles then travel along this conveyor belt. Please be careful! Then it puts the cap on the bottles. And this is where it labels them.
4 Man:	Right. I think that's everything. Is there anything else you'd like to see?
Bianchi:	Thank you. That was very interesting.
Man:	OK. Let's go up to my office and we can discuss some more …

16.2 A

Palmer:	Brian Palmer.
Steimle:	Ah Brian. It's Diana Steimle. How are things?
Palmer:	Oh hello Ms Steimle. Fine, fine.
Steimle:	I'm ringing about Mr Bianchi's visit. Has he arrived?
Palmer:	Yes, he arrived yesterday evening. I picked him up at the airport.

Steimle: Oh good. And have you explained the agenda to him?
Palmer: Yes, I did that on the way back. There was a lot of traffic, so I had plenty of time.
Steimle: Ah. Have you shown him around the company?
Palmer: Yes, I have. I did that this morning.
Steimle: And he's met the Training Manager?
Palmer: No. No, he hasn't. I haven't had time to introduce them yet.
Steimle: Right. What about the meeting with the Production Manager. Have you arranged a meeting?
Palmer: I'm afraid not. You see, Mr Zutschi wasn't in his office yesterday. I'll do that as soon as I can.
Steimle: By the way, how's the report coming on?
Palmer: Well, I've nearly finished it, but I've been quite busy with Mr Bianchi up until now.

16.3 B

1 There's a lot of competition on the domestic market, but we've launched two new products this year so things look quite good at the moment. We've spent a large part of our budget on advertising these new products and it's been a great success so far.
Internationally, we've done some market research to find out which products we can sell to the Japanese market. We hope to start selling some of our products there next year.

2 We've had another very bad year. We've had to close one of our factories. This means that over the last twelve months, 240 people have lost their jobs.
On the other hand, we've started a joint venture programme with a Hungarian company. That means everyone has to communicate in English. So we've run a number of English courses in the company ... this time during working hours.

3 We've introduced a new quality control programme. We've sent over half our staff on training courses and the results have been very good. We've not only improved the quality of our products ... the number of production faults are right down ... but we've also cut costs as well. We plan to send the rest of our staff on training courses next year.

17.1 B

Miller: You've been to New York, haven't you?
Carter: Yes, a couple of years ago. It's a great city.
Miller: I'm going to spend a couple of extra days there after the conference. I thought I'd stay on for the weekend. Any ideas what I could do?
Carter: Well, it depends what you want to do.
Miller: The usual things. You know, sightseeing, a bit of shopping. That kind of thing.
Carter: Well, how about seeing a show on Broadway. It's quite difficult to get tickets because most shows are booked up in advance. But if you go to the World Trade Center, you can often get half-price tickets for the same night.
Miller: Really, that sounds good. And what about shopping? Fifth Avenue is the place to go for shopping, isn't it?
Carter: Yes, but don't go to the big department stores. They're all over America. I prefer the boutiques in Madison Avenue.
Miller: Now where's a good place to eat out? Simon recommended the Rainbow Room.
Carter: The Rainbow Room! Forget it! It's always booked up months in advance. But you could go there for a before-dinner drink – it's definitely worth seeing. I'd go to Greenwich Village. You can get a good meal there, and it isn't nearly as expensive.
Miller: OK. And what's the best way to get around? I've heard the subway is quite dangerous.
Carter: Well, it's alright during the day. But the buses are good and you see a lot that way. Or you can walk. That's what some New Yorkers do.

17.2 A

Sikorski: Sikorski.
Dubois: Is that you, George? This is Martine. I'm just ringing to confirm the arrangements for my trip next month.
Sikorski: Ah yes. Now, would you like me to arrange accomodation?
Dubois: No, don't worry. I've booked in at the Royal Hotel. I stayed there last time and it was quite nice there.
Sikorski: Fine. Do you want me to pick you up at the airport?

Dubois: Well, that's very kind of you. If you're sure it's no trouble.
Sikorski: No, not at all. What time does your plane land?
Dubois: Twelve o'clock, I think, but I'll fax you the details.
Sikorski: OK. By the way, have you made any plans for the weekend? There's a jazz concert on the Friday. Would you like me to get tickets for it?
Dubois: Oh, that sounds great. Yes, lovely.
Sikorski: OK.

18.2 B

Recept: Good morning. HighTec.
Woman: Good morning. This is Helen Johnson from Fleeracker. I'd like to speak to Mr Noor in the Sales Department.
Recept: Sorry, what was your name?
Woman: Johnson. Helen Johnson.
Recept: Right, Ms Johnson. I'll put you through to Mr Noor.

Man: Sales Department. Noor.
Woman: My name's Helen Johnson. I'm from Fleeracker. I'm phoning about our order for the ABC 10 P and the ABC 40 S. We placed the order two months ago. The ABC 10 P arrived a couple of weeks ago, but we haven't received the 40 S yet.
Man: Yeah, just a moment. Could I have the order number?
Woman: Yes. Let me see. It's EMI 1400.
Man: EMI 1400. I'll just check that.
Woman: OK.
Man: Yeah, I'm very sorry, we've had problems with our suppliers. We're still waiting for the delivery of some of the parts.
Woman: That's all very well, but our customer is waiting too.
Man: Look, look, I'll see what I can do.
Woman: OK. But I need to know when we can expect delivery. I'll have to cancel if we don't receive it by the end of the week.
Man: I'm very sorry again. Look, can I have your phone number and I'll get back to you as soon as possible.
Woman: It's 778 9021.
Man: 778 9021. Right, Ms Johnson. I'll see what I can do.

19.1 C

Inter: Mr Green, could you tell us something about the economic forecasts for next year. For example, what will happen to housing costs?
Green: Well, there's good news for buyers. Prices won't increase. In fact, they'll fall slightly. There are different reasons for this. One is that it won't be so easy to borrow money. A second reason is that there are still a lot of empty new houses on the market.
Inter: I see. And what about food prices? Will they fall too?
Green: I'm afraid not. You see, inflation will increase, so consumer prices will rise too. I think we can expect a 3% rise in prices.
Inter: Some economists say that unemployment will rise. Are you one of these people?
Green: No, I'm not. I think it'll decrease. Trade with other countries has improved dramatically over the past year. And the increased demand for goods means that there will be more jobs.
Inter: Well, if unemployment falls, can we expect wages to fall too?
Green: No, no. The average wage will increase. Not very much, I'm afraid, but there will be a slight increase.
Inter: One final question, Mr Green. What will happen to petrol prices? Will they increase or decrease next year?
Green: That's a very difficult question to answer because we don't know what'll happen in the oil producing countries. I have a feeling that prices will go down. However, I could be wrong!
Inter: Mr Green, thank you very much for your time.
Green: Thank you.

19.2 B

1 Woman: Do you think cash'll be illegal in the next century?
  Man: Oh, I'm sure it will. You see, credit cards will replace cash, so we won't need it.

2 Woman: I expect smart cards'll take over from cash cards and all those other cards.
  Man: Really? Why do you think that?
  Woman: Well, a lot of people have them already, don't they?

3 Man: Do you think there'll be more hypermarkets in the future?
  Woman: I'm sure there won't. I mean, you have to drive to them, don't you? I think people'll shop from home. You know, from mail order catalogues or television.

4 Man: I'm certain information will become the most important commodity of the future. It is now, isn't it?

5 Woman: I don't think so many people will work in service industries.
  Man: What do you mean by service industries?
  Woman: Oh, banks, restaurants, things like that. The number's too high. 95%. No, it's too high.

6 Man: I expect I'll be an electronic immigrant in a few years time. I'll work from home with a computer.
  Woman: Really? Why do you think that?
  Man: Well, it'll be cheaper for the big companies to pay workers to stay at home.
  Woman: But what'll happen if there's a power cut?
  Man: You'll have a day off.

19.3 C

1 I'm a computer consultant. I used to work for IBM, but now I have my own business. I'm based in Connecticut, but I telecommute with clients all over the States and in London and Paris, too. I spend about 100 nights a year on the road, but I manage to keep in touch. Hotels can be a bit of a problem. Some of them don't understand the kind of things I need, you know, a desk with good lighting, a phone jack, and somewhere to plug the equipment in. But it's much better than when I first started. In fact, most of them are really computer-friendly now.

2 I work for an investment company in New York City. When I had the baby last year I worked full-time from home for five months. I then worked as a part-time telecommuter for another six months. It was great. I could work better at home, because there were no distractions. No one coming in and wanting to chat. What I liked best was that I could work for several hours at a time. Then I could take a break and be with my child. I've now gone back to work full time, but I still like to use my home office for overtime work. I do some work-ups at night and I use it for brainstorming on the weekends.

3 I work in the media relations department of a telecommunications company. I telecommute from home at least one day a week, sometimes more. The company puts through calls from the office, and I use a laptop computer to get information from their computer. I find that it's much easier to concentrate when working at home because it's quieter. It's also more convenient when I have overtime work. I don't have to get in the car on a weekend and drive 45 minutes to the office. I just go into the study, call up my reports and do it. It's really very productive.

20 D

On the whole the future of the consumer electronics industry looks bright. There are not only the well-established products but also a lot of new ones for shoppers – pocket-sized video cameras, digital tape recorders, satellite dishes and so on.

But there will be a lot of competition. For one thing, a lot of consumers already have most of the gadgets they want – so you can't impress them with the latest thing. For another thing, consumer spending has fallen steadily over the past few years.

Now, in most countries over 90% of all households own a colour television. However, there is a trend towards bigger and better pictures as people spend more of their leisure time at home. For example, over half the sets sold in Japan last year have screens bigger than 32". So I think sales will increase slightly over the next few years, certainly at least until prices for the new High Density Televisions come down.

The VCR has been a real success. The trouble is that everyone who is likely to own a VCR now has one. In Japan 80% of all households own one and the figures are similar for America and Europe. I don't think we'll see much in the way of new developments for VCRs so I think sales will continue to decline.

The situation for hi-fi is slightly different. Only 61% of all households own a stereo system. So there's still a market. And there've been lots of exciting new developments with digital sound, so I expect sales to increase steadily, at least until the end of the century.

Wordlist

accept 14.1 /əkˈsept/
accommodation 12.1 /əkɒməˈdeɪʃn/
accountant 2.1 /əˈkaʊntənt/
accounts 4.1 /əˈkaʊnts/
acknowledgement 12.3
 /əkˈnɒlɪdʒmənt/
addictive 10 C /əˈdɪktɪv/
address 2.3 /əˈdres/
administrative 2.1 /ədˈmɪnɪstrətɪv/
advance: In advance 3.3 /ɪn ədˈvɑːns/
advertise 4.2 /ˈædvətaɪz/
advertisement 4.2 /ədˈvɜːtɪsmənt/
advertising 3.2 /ˈædvətaɪzɪŋ/
advice 7.3 /ədˈvaɪs/
aerospace 3.2 /ˈeərəʊspeɪs/
afraid: I'm afraid she's ... 4.3
 /aɪm əfˈreɪd ʃiːz/
after-sales 4.1 /ɑːftəˈseɪlz/
afternoon 8.1 /ɑːftəˈnuːn/
again 18.1 /əˈgen/
age 12.2 /eɪdʒ/
agenda 16.2 /əˈdʒendə/
agent 8.1 /ˈeɪdʒənt/
ago 11.2 /əˈgəʊ/
agree: I agree 13.3 /aɪ əˈgriː/
air conditioning 9.3 /eə kənˈdɪʃnɪŋ/
airline 3.2 /ˈeəlaɪn/
airport 7.1 /ˈeəpɔːt/
all-purpose 12.2 /ɔːlˈpɜːpəs/
all right: That's all right. 1.3
 /ðæts ɔːlˈraɪt/
always 6.2 /ˈɔːlweɪz/
amount 12.3 /əˈmaʊnt/
anniversary 13.2 /ænɪˈvɜːsri/
annual 3.3 /ˈænjʊəl/
answer 5 A /ˈɑːnsə/
answering machine 13.3
 /ˈɑːnsrɪŋ məˈʃiːn/
any 12.1 /ˈeni/
anytime 13.1 /ˈenɪtaɪm/
apologize 18.3 /əˈpɒlədʒaɪz/
apology 18.3 /əˈpɒlədʒi/
appointment 4.1 /əˈpɔɪntmənt/
appreciate: We would appreciate ...
 12.3 /wi wʊd əˈpriːʃieɪt/
armchair 13.3 /ˈɑːmtʃeə/
arrange 8.2 /əˈreɪndʒ/

arrangement 8.1 /əˈreɪndʒmənt/
arrival 18.3 /əˈraɪvəl/
arrive 8.1 /əˈraɪv/
as: as ... as 13.1 /əz ... əz/
ask 4.3 /ɑːsk/
assistant 11.1 /əˈsɪstənt/
atmosphere 9.2 /ˈætməsfɪə/
attend 8.1 /əˈtend/
attention 16.1 /əˈtenʃn/
aubergine 14.3 /ˈəʊbəʒiːn/
auditor 10 C /ˈɔːdɪtə/
available 12.2 /əˈveɪləbl/
average 9.3 /ˈævrɪdʒ/
avocado 14.3 /ævəˈkɑːdəʊ/
away 8.3 /əˈweɪ/
awful 13.3 /ˈɔːfl/

background 11.1 /ˈbækgraʊnd/
bad: Not too bad 1.3 /nɒt tu ˈbæd/
baggage 12.1 /ˈbægɪdʒ/
banana 14.3 /bəˈnɑːnə/
bank 1.2 /bæŋk/
banking 3.2 /ˈbæŋkɪŋ/
bar 9.3 /bɑː/
bargain 13.1 /ˈbɑːgɪn/
barrel 19.1 /ˈbærəl/
beans 14.3 /ˈbiːnz/
become 11.1 /bɪˈkʌm/
beef 14.3 /biːf/
before 18.3 /bɪˈfɔː/
begin 6.1 /bɪˈgɪn/
behind 7.2 /bɪˈhaɪnd/
best 13.2 /best/
better 13.1 /ˈbetə/
between 7.2 /bɪˈtwiːn/
bicycle 12.2 /ˈbaɪsɪkl/
big 13.2 /bɪg/
birthday 7.1 /ˈbɜːθdeɪ/
bit: a bit 14.3 /ə ˈbɪt/
black 1.3 /blæk/
black and white 13.3 /blæk ən ˈwaɪt/
book (v) 7.2 /bʊk/
bookcase 13.3 /ˈbʊkkeɪs/
boss 6.3 /bɒs/
branch 1.2 /brɑːntʃ/
brand 16.3 /brænd/
break (n) 6.1 /breɪk/

break (v): break down 18.1
 /breɪk ˈdaʊn/
breakfast 6.2 /ˈbrekfəst/
brochure 3.3 /ˈbrəʊʃə/
bus 17.1 /bʌs/
business card 2.3 /ˈbɪznəs kɑːd/
business trip 4.3 /ˈbɪznəs trɪp/
business: on business 9.1 /ɒn ˈbɪznəs/
busy 4.3 /ˈbɪzi/
buy 4.2 /baɪ/

C.V. (Curriculum Vitae) 4.2
 /siːˈviː/ (/kərɪkjələm ˈviːtaɪ/)
cab 17.1 /kæb/
call (v) 4.3 /kɔːl/
call: Please call me ... 1.1
 /pliːz kɔːl mi/
calling: Who's calling please? 4.3
 /huːz ˈkɔːlɪŋ pliːz/
canteen 4.1 /kænˈtiːn/
car 3.2 /kɑː/
career 11.1 /kəˈrɪə/
careful: Be careful 16.1 /bi ˈkeəfl/
case 18.3 /keɪs/
cash 19.2 /kæʃ/
catalogue 4.2 /ˈkætəlɒg/
catch 8.1 /kætʃ/
central 9.3 /ˈsentrəl/
certain: I'm certain ... 19.2
 /aɪm ˈsɜːtn/
certainly 4.3 /ˈsɜːtnli/
chain 16.3 /tʃeɪn/
chair 13.3 /tʃeə/
cheap 13.1 /tʃiːp/
check (v) 18.1 /tʃek/
check out 17.1 /ˈtʃek aʊt/
chemicals 3.2 /ˈkemɪklz/
cheque 4.2 /tʃek/
chicken 14.3 /ˈtʃɪkɪn/
children 12.2 /ˈtʃɪldrən/
choice 9.3 /tʃɔɪs/
city 1.2 /ˈsiti/
classic 12.2 /ˈklæsɪk/
clerical 2.1 /ˈklerɪkl/
clerk 2.1 /klɑːk/
clock 12.2 /klɒk/
close (adj) 9.3 /kləʊs/

clothing 3.2 /ˈkləʊðɪŋ/
coffee machine 13.3 /ˈkɒfi məʃiːn/
cold 9.1 /kəʊld/
colleague 6.3 /ˈkɒliːg/
colour 12.2 /ˈkʌlə/
come 9.1 /kʌm/
come: come out of 4.1 /kʌm aʊt əv/
comment 12.3 /ˈkɒment/
commercial (adj) 4.2 /kəˈmɜːʃl/
commercial (n) 13.2 /kəˈmɜːʃl/
commodity 19.2 /kəˈmɒditi/
common 14.1 /ˈkɒmən/
commuting 6.3 /kəˈmjuːtɪŋ/
complain 20 A /kəmˈpleɪn/
component 12.2 /kəmˈpəʊnənt/
computer 3.2 /kəmˈpjuːtə/
computer hire 9.3 /kəmpjuːtə ˈhaɪə/
concert 17.1 /ˈkɒnsət/
condition: in good condition 18.3
     /ɪn gʊd kənˈdɪʃn/
conference 1.2 /ˈkɒnfrəns/
confirm 12.3 /kənˈfɜːm/
connect: Could you connect me
     with ...? 4.3
     /kʊd ju kəˈnekt mi wɪð/
consumer 16.3 /kənˈsjuːmə/
consumer electronics 3.2
     /kənsjuːmə elɪkˈtrɒnɪks/
consumption 16.3 /kənˈsʌmpʃn/
contact (n) 9.2 /ˈkɒntækt/
contact (v): Please contact me 4.2
     /pliːz ˈkɒntækt mi/
contract (n) 13.1 /ˈkɒntrækt/
convenient 8.3 /kənˈviːnɪənt/
copy (4.2) /ˈkɒpi/
cordless 13.3 /ˈkɔːdləs/
cost (v) 12.2 /kɒst/
cost (n) 18.3 /kɒst/
cost of living 19.2 /kɒst əv ˈlɪvɪŋ/
cough 7.3 /kɒf/
could you ... 7.1 /ˈkʊd juː/
couple: couple of days 16.2
     /kʌpl əv ˈdeɪz/
course: Of course 4.3 /əv ˈkɔːs/
course: main course 14.3 /meɪn ˈkɔːs/
credit card 7.1 /ˈkredɪt kɑːd/
crowded 9.1 /ˈkraʊdɪd/
cupboard 13.3 /ˈkʌbəd/
currency 12.2 /ˈkʌrənsi/
current affairs 15 C /kʌrənt əˈfeəz/
customer 4.2 /ˈkʌstəmə/
cycle (v) 7.3 /ˈsaɪkl/

daily 7.2 /ˈdeɪli/
damage 18.3 /ˈdæmɪdʒ/
dangerous 14.1 /ˈdeɪndʒrəs/

date: delivery dates 4.2
     /dɪˈlɪvəri deɪts/
day 6.2 /deɪ/
day: day off 14.2 /deɪ ˈɒf/
deadline 7.2 /ˈdedlaɪn/
deal: deal with 4.2 /ˈdiːl wɪð/
decision 7.2 /dɪˈsɪʒn/
decrease (v) 19.1 /dɪˈkriːs/
delivery 4.1 /dɪˈlɪvəri/
deluxe 12.2 /dɪˈlʌks/
dentist 14.2 /ˈdentɪst/
department 2.1 /dɪˈpɑːtmənt/
description 12.3 /dɪsˈkrɪpʃn/
desk 13.3 /desk/
dessert 14.3 /dɪˈzɜːt/
details 3.3 /ˈdiːteɪlz/
develop 4.2 /dɪˈveləp/
diary 8.1 /ˈdaɪəri/
dictation 11.3 /dɪkˈteɪʃn/
difficult 14.1 /ˈdɪfɪklt/
dinner 6.2 /ˈdɪnə/
directory 4.1 /dɪˈrektəri/
disappointing 9.2 /dɪsəˈpɔɪntɪŋ/
discount (n) 4.2 /ˈdɪskaʊnt/
discuss 8.1 /dɪsˈkʌs/
discussion 17.3 /dɪsˈkʌʃn/
dish 14.3 /dɪʃ/
disk 18.1 /dɪsk/
dispatch (n) 4.2 /dɪsˈpætʃ/
display 12.2 /dɪsˈpleɪ/
distance 12.2 /ˈdɪstəns/
distribution 5 C /dɪstrɪˈbjuːʃn/
district 9.3 /ˈdɪstrɪkt/
do: do overtime 7.2 /du ˈəʊvətaɪm/
do: do the filing 7.1 /duː ðə ˈfaɪlɪŋ/
doctor 14.2 /ˈdɒktə/
domestic appliance 5 C
     /dəmestɪk əˈplaɪəns/
dramatically 19.1 /drəˈmætɪkli/
drink (n) 3.2 /drɪŋk/
drink (v) 7.3 /drɪŋk/

easy 12.2 /ˈiːzi/
eat 6.2 /iːt/
education 11.1 /edʒʊˈkeɪʃn/
electronic 13.3 /elɪkˈtrɒnɪk/
electronics 3.2 /elɪkˈtrɒnɪks/
elevator 4.1 /ˈeləveɪtə/
else: anything else 16.1 /ˈeniθɪŋ els/
employ 5 C /ɪmˈplɔɪ/
employee 3.1 /emplɔɪˈiː/
enclose: We enclose our brochure 3.3
     /wi ɪŋkləʊz aʊə ˈbrəʊʃə/
enclosed: Please find enclosed ... 4.2
     /pliːz faɪnd ɪŋˈkləʊzd/
energy 3.2 /ˈenədʒi/

engineer 2.1 /endʒɪˈnɪə/
engineering 3.2 /endʒɪˈnɪərɪŋ/
enjoy 6.3 /ɪnˈdʒɔɪ/
enough 9.2 /ɪˈnʌf/
enquiry 4.2 /ɪŋˈkwaɪəri/
entertain 6.2 /entəˈteɪn/
entertainment 17.1 /entəˈteɪnmənt/
environment 19.3 /ɪnˈvaɪrənmənt/
equipment 3.2 /ɪkˈwɪpmənt/
essential 13.3 /ɪˈsenʃəl/
evening 6.2 /ˈiːvnɪŋ/
event 9.2 /ɪˈvent/
exactly: when exactly 14.2
     /wen ɪgˈzæktli/
excellent 9.1 /ˈeksələnt/
Excuse me 1.1 /ɪksˈkjuːz mi/
exercise 7.2 /ˈeksəsaɪz/
exhibition 9.2 /eksɪˈbɪʃn/
expect 18.2 /ɪksˈpekt/
expensive 13.1 /ɪksˈpensɪv/
experience 4.2 /ɪksˈpɪərɪəns/
explain 16.2 /ɪksˈpleɪn/
export (n) 2.1 /ˈekspɔːt/
export (v) 3.3 /ɪksˈpɔːt/
extension 7.1 /ɪksˈtenʃn/

facility 9.3 /fəˈsɪlɪti/
factory 4.2 /ˈfæktri/
fair (n) 8.1 /feə/
fairly 14.3 /ˈfeəli/
fall (v) 19.1 /fɔːl/
family 6.3 /ˈfæmli/
fantastic 9.2 /fænˈtæstɪk/
far 9.2 /fɑː/
fashionable 12.2 /ˈfæʃnəbl/
fast 13.2 /fɑːst/
feel 7.3 /fiːl/
few 9.2 /fjuː/
fifth (ord) 4.1 /fɪfθ/
file (n) 13.3 /faɪl/
file (v) 18.1 /faɪl/
filing 7.1 /ˈfaɪlɪŋ/
filing cabinet 13.3 /ˈfaɪlɪŋ kæbɪnət/
financial services 3.2
     /faɪnænʃl ˈsɜːvɪsɪz/
find: find out about 17.2
     /faɪnd aʊt əˈbaʊt/
fine: That's fine 8.2 /ðæts ˈfaɪn/
finish 6.1 /ˈfɪnɪʃ/
first (ord) 4.1 /fɜːst/
fish 14.3 /fɪʃ/
fit 7.3 /fɪt/
fitness centre 9.3 /ˈfɪtnəs sentə/
flight 9.1 /flaɪt/
floor 4.1 /flɔː/
florist 9.3 /ˈflɒrɪst/

fluent 11.1 /ˈfluːənt/
fly (v) 8.1 /flaɪ/
foggy 9.1 /ˈfɒgi/
food 3.2 /fuːd/
foot: on foot 17.1 /ɒn ˈfʊt/
forecast 19.1 /ˈfɔːkɑːst/
forget 13.2 /fəˈget/
fortune 6.3 /ˈfɔːtʃuːn/
fourth (ord) 4.1 /fɔːθ/
frame 12.2 /freɪm/
free 13.1 /friː/
free: free time 7.2 /friː ˈtaɪm/
free: Are you free on ...? 8.2
  /ɑː ju ˈfriː ɒn/
fridge 13.3 /frɪdʒ/
friendly 6.3 /ˈfrendli/
function 12.2 /ˈfʌŋkʃn/
furniture 13.2 /ˈfɜːnɪtʃə/
future 12.2 /ˈfjuːtʃə/

game 17.3 /geɪm/
general 16.3 /ˈdʒenrəl/
get: Can I get you anything? 9.1
  /kæn aɪ get ju ˈeniθɪŋ/
get: get on with s.o. 11.3
  /get ɒn wɪð ˈsʌmwʌn/
get: get angry 7.2 /get ˈæŋgri/
get: get up 6.2 /get ʌp/
get: get to the office 6.2
  /get tə ðiː ˈɒfɪs/
get: get back 16.1 /get bæk/
gift 15 C /gɪft/
give 3.3 /gɪv/
go: go on a trip 6.2 /gəʊ ɒn ə ˈtrɪp/
go: go home 6.2 /gəʊ ˈhəʊm/
go: go to bed 6.2 /gəʊ tə ˈbed/
go: go down 19.1 /gəʊ ˈdaʊn/
go: go up 19.1 /gəʊ ˈʌp/
good 13.1 /gʊd/
goods 3.3 /gʊdz/
great 6.3 /greɪt/
green 12.2 /griːn/
greet 5 A /griːt/
grey 12.2 /greɪ/
grow 7.3 /grəʊ/
guarantee 13.1 /gærənˈtiː/
guest 14.1 /gest/

hairdresser 9.3 /ˈheədresə/
happy 8.3 /ˈhæpi/
hard (adv): work hard 7.3
  /wɜːk ˈhɑːd/
hard (adj): hard work 9.2
  /hɑːd ˈwɜːk/
hardly ever 6.2 /ˈhɑːdli ˈevə/
hate 6.3 /heɪt/

have to 7.2 /ˈhæv tuː/
have: have dinner 8.1 /hæv ˈdɪnə/
have: Have a nice weekend 1.3
  /hæv ə naɪs wiːˈkend/
have: Have a seat 1.3 /hæv ə ˈsiːt/
have: have breakfast 6.2
  /hæv ˈbrekfəst/
headquarters 3.1 /hedˈkwɔːtəz/
health 7.2 /helθ/
help (n): Thank you for your help 1.3
  /θæŋk ju fə jɔː ˈhelp/
help (v) 4.2 /help/
herbal teas 7.3 /hɜːbl ˈtiːz/
hesitate 4.2 /ˈhezɪteɪt/
high 13.2 /haɪ/
high-tec 12.2 /haɪˈtek/
hobby 7.3 /ˈhɒbi/
hold: Hold the line, please 2.2
  /həʊld ðə ˈlaɪn pliːz/
holiday: on holiday 4.3 /ɒn ˈhɒlɪdeɪ/
home 7.3 /həʊm/
hospitality 17.3 /hɒspəˈtæləti/
host 14.1 /həʊst/
hot 14.3 /hɒt/
hot line 13.1 /ˈhɒt laɪn/
hotel 3.2 /həʊˈtel/
hours 6.3 /ˈaʊəz/
housewife 15 C /ˈhaʊswaɪf/
housing 19.1 /ˈhaʊzɪŋ/
how: How do you do? 1.1
  /haʊ də ju ˈduː/
how: How much is it? 12.2
  /haʊ ˈmʌtʃ ɪz ɪt/
how: How are you? 1.2 /haʊ ɑː juː/
how: How was ... 9.2 /ˈhaʊ wəz/
how: How about ... 1.3 /haʊ əˈbaʊt/
husband 15 C /ˈhʌzbənd/
hypermarket 19.2 /ˈhaɪpəmɑːkɪt/

ice cream 14.3 /ˈaɪs kriːm/
idea: Good idea 13.3 /gʊd aɪˈdɪə/
ideal 9.3 /aɪˈdɪəl/
ill 4.3 /ɪl/
image 12.2 /ˈɪmɪdʒ/
immigrant 19.2 /ˈɪmɪgrənt/
impolite 14.1 /ɪmpəˈlaɪt/
import (v) 3.3 /ɪmˈpɔːt/
import (n) 19.1 /ˈɪmpɔːt/
important 13.3 /ɪmˈpɔːtənt/
included 13.1 /ɪŋˈkluːdɪd/
inconvenience 18.3 /ɪŋkənˈviːnɪəns/
increase (v) 4.2 /ɪŋˈkriːs/
inflation 19.1 /ɪnˈfleɪʃn/
information 4.2 /ɪnfəˈmeɪʃn/
inserts (n) 15 C /ˈɪnsɜːts/
install 16.3 /ɪnˈstɔːl/

insurance 3.2 /ɪnˈʃʊərəns/
intend 18.3 /ɪnˈtend/
interest 19.1 /ˈɪntrəst/
interested: interested in 13.2
  /ˈɪntrəstɪd ɪn/
interesting 6.3 /ˈɪntrəstɪŋ/
interpreter 9.3 /ɪnˈtɜːprɪtə/
interview (n) 14.2 /ˈɪntəvjuː/
introduce 5 A /ɪntrəˈdjuːs/
invest 16.3 /ɪnˈvest/
investment 16.3 /ɪnˈvestmənt/
invitation 14.1 /ɪnvɪˈteɪʃn/
invite 14.1 /ɪnˈvaɪt/
invoice 4.2 /ˈɪnvɔɪs/
item 12.3 /ˈaɪtəm/

job 2.1 /dʒɒb/
join 11.1 /dʒɔɪn/
journal 4.2 /ˈdʒɜːnl/
journey 9.1 /ˈdʒɜːni/
junior 11.1 /ˈdʒuːnɪə/
just 16.2 /dʒʌst/

kind: That's very kind of you 14.2
  /ðæts veri ˈkaɪnd əv juː/
kind: It's a kind of ... 14.3
  /ɪts ə ˈkaɪnd əv/
know-how 10 C /ˈnəʊ haʊ/
know: Do you know ... ? 1.3
  /du ju ˈnəʊ/
know: Please let me know ... 8.1
  /pliːz let mi ˈnəʊ/

label: private label 16.3
  /praɪvət ˈleɪbl/
lamb 14.3 /læmb/
large 13.2 /lɑːdʒ/
last (adj) 7.3 /lɑːst/
late 6.2 /leɪt/
latest 14.2 /ˈleɪtəst/
laugh 7.3 /lɑːf/
lawyer 2.1 /ˈlɔɪə/
leading 16.3 /ˈliːdɪŋ/
learn 9.2 /lɜːn/
leather 12.2 /ˈleðə/
leave 6.1 /liːv/
left 4.1 /left/
left: on the left 4.1 /ɒn ðə ˈleft/
left: turn left 4.1 /tɜːn ˈleft/
leisure 9.3 /ˈleʒə/
lend 7.1 /lend/
less 7.2 /les/
let: Please let me know ... 8.1
  /pliːz let mi ˈnəʊ/
let: Let's see 18.2 /lets ˈsiː/
let: Let's ... 13.3 /lets/

letter of credit 12.3 /ˈletə əv ˈkredɪt/
like (v) 6.3 /laɪk/
like: What was it like? 9.2
   /wɒt wəz ɪt ˈlaɪk/
like: I'd like to ... 8.2 /aɪd ˈlaɪk tuː/
like: It's like ... 14.3 /ɪts ˈlaɪk/
like: Would you like me to ... 17.2
   /wʊd ju ˈlaɪk mi tuː/
like: Would you like to ...? 14.2
   /wʊd ju ˈlaɪk tuː/
line 16.3 /laɪn/
line: Hold the line, please 2.2
   /həʊld ðə ˈlaɪn pliːz/
live (v) 11.1 /lɪv/
living standards 19.2 /ˈlɪvɪŋ stændədz/
local 14.1 /ˈləʊkl/
location 9.3 /ləʊˈkeɪʃn/
long 7.2 /lɒŋ/
look: I look forward to hearing from
   you 4.2
   /aɪ lʊk ˈfɔːwəd tə ˈhɪərɪŋ frɒm juː/
look: look round 9.1 /lʊk raʊnd/
look: I'm looking for ... 4.1
   /aɪm ˈlʊkɪŋ fə/
look: I'll look into it 18.2
   /aɪl lʊk ˈɪntu ɪt/
look: I'll look forward to it 14.2
   /aɪl lʊk ˈfɔːwəd tu ɪt/
lot 7.2 /lɒt/
lovely 17.3 /ˈlʌvliː/
low 13.2 /ləʊ/
luggage 12.1 /ˈlʌgɪdʒ/
lunch 4.3 /lʌntʃ/

machinery 16.1 /məˈʃiːnəri/
magazine 4.2 /mægəˈziːn/
maintenance 13.1 /ˈmeɪntənəns/
major 16.3 /ˈmeɪdʒə/
make 3.2 /meɪk/
make: make photocopies 7.1
   /meɪk ˈfəʊtəkɒpiːz/
make: make a mistake 7.2
   /meɪk ə mɪsˈteɪk/
make: make coffee 7.1 /meɪk ˈkɒfi/
make: make a decision 7.2
   /meɪk ə dɪˈsɪʒn/
make: I can't make Friday 14.2
   /aɪ kɑːnt meɪk ˈfraɪdeɪ/
man-made 12.2 /mænˈmeɪd/
manual (adj) 13.3 /ˈmænjʊəl/
manual (n) 18.1 /ˈmænjʊəl/
manufacture 3.2 /mænjəˈfæktʃə/
map 3.1 /mæp/
market (n) 3.3 /ˈmɑːkɪt/
market (v) 4.2 /ˈmɑːkɪt/
market research 16.3 /mɑːkɪt rɪˈsɜːtʃ/

marketing 2.1 /ˈmɑːkɪtɪŋ/
matter: in this matter 18.3
   /ɪn ðɪs ˈmætə/
meal 17.1 /miːl/
meet 6.2 /miːt/
meet: Pleased to meet you 1.1
   /pliːzd tə ˈmiːt juː/
meet: Nice to meet you 1.1
   /naɪs tə ˈmiːt juː/
meet: meet a deadline 7.2
   /miːt ə ˈdedlaɪn/
meeting 4.3 /ˈmiːtɪŋ/
melon 14.3 /ˈmelən/
memo 16.2 /ˈmeməʊ/
menu 14.3 /ˈmenjuː/
message 4.3 /ˈmesɪdʒ/
mind: I don't mind 6.3
   /aɪ dəʊnt maɪnd/
miss (v) 19.3 /mɪs/
mistake 7.2 /mɪsˈteɪk/
mix-up 18.2 /ˈmɪksʌp/
model 12.2 /ˈmɒdl/
modern 13.2 /ˈmɒdn/
moment: Just a moment, please 2.2
   /dʒʌst ə ˈməʊmənt pliːz/
money 12.1 /ˈmʌni/
money-back 13.1 /ˈmʌnibæk/
month 6.2 /mʌnθ/
more 7.2 /mɔː/
morning 8.1 /ˈmɔːnɪŋ/
mountain bike 12.2 /ˈmaʊntɪn baɪk/
move 11.1 /muːv/
mushroom 14.3 /ˈmʌʃrʊm/
music 17.1 /ˈmjuːzɪk/
must 7.2 /mʌst/

name 1.1 /neɪm/
nationality 3.1 /næʃˈnælɪti/
near 7.3 /nɪə/
need 7.2 /niːd/
new 9.2 /njuː/
next to 4.1 /ˈnekst tuː/
nice: That would be nice 9.1
   /ðæt wʊd bi ˈnaɪs/
nice: That sounds nice 14.2
   /ðæt saʊndz ˈnaɪs/
normally 6.2 /ˈnɔːməli/
not at all 7.1 /nɒt ət ˈɔːl/
note (n) 4.1 /nəʊt/
notice (v) 18.3 /ˈnəʊtɪs/
nylon 12.2 /ˈnaɪlɒn/

occupation 2.1 /ɒkjəˈpeɪʃn/
offer (v) 4.2 /ˈɒfə/
offer (n) 13.2 /ˈɒfə/
office 1.2 /ˈɒfɪs/

oil 3.2 /ɔɪl/
on-site 13.1 /ɒnˈsaɪt/
once 6.2 /wʌns/
only 13.1 /ˈəʊnli/
open (v) 7.1 /ˈəʊpən/
open (adj) 6.1 /ˈəʊpən/
opinion: in my opinion 13.3
   /ɪn maɪ əˈpɪnjən/
opposite 4.1 /ˈɒpəzɪt/
order (n) 4.2 /ˈɔːdə/
order (v) 18.1 /ˈɔːdə/
Order Processing 18.1
   /ɔːdə ˈprəʊsesɪŋ/
organize 4.2 /ˈɔːgənaɪz/
other 13.2 /ˈʌðə/
overseas 5 C /əʊvəˈsiːz/
overtime 7.2 /ˈəʊvətaɪm/
own: on my own 6.3 /ɒn maɪ ˈəʊn/

pack 18.3 /pæk/
package 13.1 /ˈpækɪdʒ/
packaging 16.3 /ˈpækɪdʒɪŋ/
paid 10 C /peɪd/
part-time 11.2 /pɑːtˈtaɪm/
pasta 14.3 /ˈpæstə/
pay: pay attention to 16.1
   /peɪ əˈtenʃn tuː/
payment 4.2 /ˈpeɪmənt/
performance 10 C /pəˈfɔːməns/
perks 6.3 /pɜːks/
personnel 4.2 /pɜːsnˈel/
petrol 19.1 /ˈpetrəl/
photocopy 7.1 /ˈfəʊtəkɒpi/
pick: pick s.o. up 17.2
   /pɪk sʌmwʌn ˈʌp/
picture 13.3 /ˈpɪktʃə/
piece 7.1 /piːs/
pity: That's a pity 14.2 /ðæts ə ˈpɪti/
place: place an order 18.2
   /pleɪs ən ˈɔːdə/
plan (n) 4.1 /plæn/
plane 8.1 /pleɪn/
plans 8.1 /plænz/
plant (v) 7.3 /plɑːnt/
plant (n) 13.3 /plɑːnt/
plant (n) 16.3 /plɑːnt/
pleased 9.2 /pliːzd/
pleasure: It would be a great pleasure
   14.2 /ɪt wʊd bi ə greɪt ˈpleʒə/
polite 14.2 /pəˈlaɪt/
politics 9.1 /ˈpɒlɪtɪks/
pool 9.3 /puːl/
popular 14.3 /ˈpɒpjələ/
position 11.2 /pəˈzɪʃn/
possible: as soon as possible 7.1
   /əz suːn əz ˈpɒsəbl/

possible: it's possible ... 19.2 /ɪts 'pɒsəbl/

post (n) 7.1 /pəʊst/

prawn 14.3 /prɔːn/

prediction 20 A /prɪ'dɪkʃn/

prefer 10 C /prɪ'fɜː/

prepare 7.2 /prɪ'peə/

present (n) 13.2 /'prezənt/

present: at present 3.3 /ət 'prezənt/

price list 4.2 /'praɪs lɪst/

price 12.2 /praɪs/

print: out of print 18.1 /aʊt əv 'prɪnt/

printer 18.1 /'prɪntə/

problem 4.2 /'prɒbləm/

problem: No problem 7.1 /nəʊ 'prɒbləm/

produce (v) 3.2 /prə'djuːs/

production 4.2 /prə'dʌkʃn/

productive 9.2 /prə'dʌktɪv/

professional 2.1 /prə'feʃnl/

promise 20 A /'prɒmɪs/

properly 18.3 /'prɒpəli/

publisher 4.2 /'pʌblɪʃə/

purchase 15 C /'pɜːtʃəs/

purchasing 4.2 /'pɜːtʃəsɪŋ/

put: Could you put me through to ... ? 4.3 /kʊd ju pʊt mi 'θruː tuː/

qualification 11.1 /kwɒlɪfɪ'keɪʃn/

quality: Quality Control 16.3 /'kwɒlɪti kəntrəʊl/

quantity 12.3 /'kwɒntɪti/

question: if you have any further questions 6.1 /ɪf ju hæv eni fɜːðə 'kwestʃənz/

quiet 9.3 /'kwaɪət/

quite 14.3 /kwaɪt/

radio 13.3 /'reɪdiəʊ/

range 12.2 /reɪndʒ/

rapidly 19.1 /'ræpɪdli/

rarely 6.2 /'reəli/

rather: I'd rather not 7.1 /aɪd 'rɑːðə nɒt/

really 13.3 /'rɪəli/

really: not really 9.1 /nɒt 'rɪəli/

receive 18.2 /rɪ'siːv/

recent 17.3 /'riːsənt/

reception 14.2 /rɪ'sepʃn/

receptionist 2.1 /rɪ'sepʃnɪst/

recommend 11.1 /rekə'mend/

recommendation 15 C /rekəmen'deɪʃn/

ref. 7.1 /ref/

refer: I refer to ... 4.2 /aɪ rɪ'fɜː tuː/

refund 18.2 /'riːfʌnd/

refuse 15 A /rɪ'fjuːz/

regards: Give my regards to ... 17.3 /gɪv maɪ rɪ'gɑːdz tuː/

relax 7.3 /rɪ'læks/

repeat: Can you repeat that, please? 2.2 /kæn ju rɪ'piːt ðæt pliːz/

replace 18.1 /rɪ'pleɪs/

report (n) 6.2 /rɪ'pɔːt/

represent 11.1 /reprɪ'zent/

representative 4.2 /reprɪ'zentətɪv/

reputation 15 C /repjə'teɪʃn/

require 4.2 /rɪ'kwaɪə/

requirement 16.1 /rɪ'kwaɪəmənt/

Research and Development 4.2 /rɪsɜːtʃ ən dɪ'veləpmənt/

reserve 7.1 /rɪ'zɜːv/

responsibility 11.3 /rɪspɒnsə'bɪləti/

rest 18.1 /rest/

restaurant 3.2 /'restərɒnt/

retail 12.2 /'riːteɪl/

review 16.3 /rɪ'vjuː/

rice 14.3 /raɪs/

rich 14.3 /rɪtʃ/

right 4.1 /raɪt/

right: That's right 3.1 /ðæts raɪt/

right: on the right 4.1 /ɒn ðə 'raɪt/

rise (v) 19.1 /raɪz/

robot 19.2 /'rəʊbɒt/

room 7.1 /ruːm/

room 13.3 /ruːm/

room service 9.3 /'ruːm sɜːvɪs/

routine 6.1 /ru'tiːn/

safety 12.2 /'seɪfti/

salary 6.3 /'sæləri/

sale 13.2 /seɪl/

sales 2.1 /seɪlz/

sauna 9.3 /'sɔːnə/

save 13.1 /seɪv/

say 5 A /seɪ/

schedule 8.1 /'ʃedjuːl/

school 11.1 /skuːl/

science 15 C /'saɪəns/

seat 1.3 /siːt/

second (ord) 4.1 /'sekənd/

secretary 2.1 /'sekrətri/

security 16.1 /sə'kjʊərəti/

see: Nice to see you again 1.2 /naɪs tə 'siː ju əgen/

see: See you on Friday 1.3 /siː ju ɒn 'fraɪdeɪ/

see: I'll see what I can do 18.2 /aɪl siː wɒt aɪ kən 'duː/

seem 18.2 /siːm/

selection 13.2 /sə'lekʃn/

sell 3.2 /sel/

seminar 9.2 /'semɪnɑː/

send 3.3 /send/

senior 11.1 /'siːnɪə/

service 3.2 /'sɜːvɪs/

service 9.1 /'sɜːvɪs/

Shall I ... 17.2 /ʃəl 'aɪ/

shift 6.3 /ʃɪft/

shop 9.3 /ʃɒp/

shopping 17.1 /'ʃɒpɪŋ/

shopping arcade 9.3 /'ʃɒpɪŋ ɑːkeɪd/

short 12.2 /ʃɔːt/

should 7.3 /ʃʊd/

show 16.2 /ʃəʊ/

shower 7.1 /'ʃaʊə/

sightseeing 17.1 /'saɪtsiːɪŋ/

sign 16.1 /saɪn/

similar 3.3 /'sɪmɪlə/

single room 7.1 /sɪŋgl 'ruːm/

size 12.2 /saɪz/

sleep (v) 7.3 /sliːp/

slightly 19.1 /'slaɪtli/

slowly 19.1 /'sləʊli/

small 5 C /smɔːl/

smart card 19.2 /'smɑːt kɑːd/

smoke 7.2 /sməʊk/

sofa 13.3 /'səʊfə/

soft drink 3.2 /sɒft 'drɪŋk/

software package 13.1 /'sɒftweə pækɪdʒ/

solution 14.1 /sə'luːʃn/

some 12.1 /sʌm/

sometimes 6.2 /'sʌmtaɪmz/

sorry: I'm sorry 1.1 /aɪm 'sɒri/

sorry: I'm sorry to hear that 9.1 /aɪm sɒri tə 'hɪə ðæt/

sound: That sounds nice 14.2 /ðæt saʊndz 'naɪs/

soup 14.3 /suːp/

speak: I'd like to speak to ... 2.2 /aɪd laɪk tə 'spiːk tuː/

speak: Can I speak to ... ? 2.2 /kæn aɪ 'spiːk tuː/

speaking: Who's speaking please? 2.2 /huːz 'spiːkɪŋ pliːz/

speciality 14.3 /speʃi'æləti/

speed 12.2 /spiːd/

spell: How do you spell ... ? 2.2 /haʊ də ju 'spel/

spell: Can you spell ... ? 2.2 /kæn ju 'spel/

spend: spend time 7.1 /spend 'taɪm/

spend: spend money 13.3 /spend 'mʌni/

spicy 14.3 /'spaɪsi/

sports centre 9.3 /'spɔːts sentə/

sportswear 12.2 /'spɔːtsweə/

staff 6.1 /stɑːf/
stand (n) 12.1 /stænd/
stand (v) : Stand back 16.1
　/stænd 'bæk/
standard 12.2 /'stændəd/
start 6.1 /stɑːt/
starter 14.3 /'stɑːtə/
stay 8.2 /steɪ/
stew 14.3 /stjuː/
stock 12.2 /stɒk/
stop 16.1 /stɒp/
storage 13.3 /'stɔːrɪdʒ/
strange 18.3 /streɪndʒ/
strawberry 14.3 /'strɔːbri/
stress 7.2 /stres/
stressful 9.2 /'stresfl/
study 11.1 /'stʌdi/
subsidiary 5 C /sʌb'sɪdjəri/
subway 17.1 /'sʌbweɪ/
successful 9.2 /sək'sesfl/
sugar 1.3 /'ʃʊgə/
suit 8.1 /suːt/
suit: Does ... suit you? 8.2
　/dʌz ... suːt juː/
suitable 12.2 /'suːtəbl/
suitcase 12.1 /'suːtkeɪs/
summer 19.1 /'sʌmə/
supervisor 2.1 /'suːpəvaɪzə/
supplier 18.2 /sə'plaɪə/
support 13.1 /sə'pɔːt/
sure 7.1 /ʃɔː/
sure: I'm sure ... 19.2 /aɪm 'ʃɔː/
surprised 14.1 /sə'praɪzd/
sweet 14.3 /swiːt/

take: take a course 11.1 /teɪk ə 'kɔːs/
take: take up a hobby 7.3
　/teɪk ʌp ə 'hɒbi/
take: take the elevator 4.1
　/teɪk ðɪ 'eləveɪtə/
take: Can I take a message? 4.3
　/kæn aɪ teɪk ə 'mesɪdʒ/
take: take the train 6.2 /teɪk ðə 'treɪn/
take: It takes an hour 7.3
　/ɪt teɪks ən 'aʊə/
talk 7.3 /tɔːk/
talk: Nice to talk to you 1.3
　/naɪs tə 'tɔːk tə juː/
tea 6.2 /tiː/
technical 2.1 /'teknɪkl/
technology 7.2 /tek'nɒlədʒi/
telecommunications 3.2
　/telɪkəmjuːnɪ'keɪʃnz/
telefax 2.3 /'telɪfæks/
telephone 2.2 /'telɪfəʊn/
television 13.3 /telɪ'vɪʒn/

temperature 12.2 /'temprətʃə/
tennis 9.3 /'tenɪs/
terrible 7.3 /'terɪbl/
terrific 6.3 /tə'rɪfɪk/
test (v) 18.3 /test/
theatre 17.1 /'θɪətə/
third (ord) 4.1 /θɜːd/
this is ... 1.3 /'ðɪs ɪz/
throw: throw away 18.1 /θrəʊ ə'weɪ/
time 6.2 /taɪm/
tiring 9.2 /'taɪərɪŋ/
tomorrow 6.2 /tə'mɒrəʊ/
tonight 12.1 /tə'naɪt/
topic 14.1 /'tɒpɪk/
total 12.3 /'təʊtəl/
touch 16.1 /'tʌtʃ/
tour 12.2 /tʊə/
tourism 3.2 /'tʊərɪzm/
tournament 17.2 /'tɔːnəmənt/
town 5 C /taʊn/
trade 4.2 /'treɪd/
trade fair 9.2 /'treɪd feə/
train (n) 6.2 /treɪn/
train (v) 11.1 /treɪn/
training 11.1 /'treɪnɪŋ/
training course 9.2 /'treɪnɪŋ kɔːs/
translation 9.3 /træns'leɪʃn/
transport 17.1 /'trænspɔːt/
travel (n) 3.2 /'trævl/
travel (v) 7.2 /'trævl/
tree 7.3 /triː/
trip 8.1 /trɪp/
trouble: If it's no trouble 17.2
　/ɪf ɪts nəʊ 'trʌbl/
truck 3.1 /trʌk/
try 18.2 /traɪ/
turn: turn right 4.1 /tɜːn 'raɪt/
turn: turn on 18.3 /tɜːn 'ɒn/
twice 6.2 /twaɪs/
type 7.1 /taɪp/
typewriter 13.3 /'taɪpraɪtə/
typist 2.1 /'taɪpɪst/

uncomfortable 13.3 /ʌn'kʌmftəbl/
unemployment 19.1
　/ʌnɪm'plɔɪmənt/
unfortunately 8.3 /ʌn'fɔːtʃənətli/
unit price 12.3 /juːnɪt 'praɪs/
until 7.3 /ʌn'tɪl/
urgent 7.1 /'ɜːdʒənt/
use (v) 6.2 /juːz/
useful 9.2 /'juːsfl/
usually 6.2 /'juːʒəli/

vacation 4.3 /və'keɪʃn/
vegetable 14.3 /'vedʒtəbl/

vehicle 3.2 /'vɪəkl/
very 9.2 /'veri/
video 16.2 /'vɪdɪəʊ/
visit (v) 8.1 /'vɪzɪt/
visitor 6.2 /'vɪzɪtə/

wages 19.1 /'weɪdʒɪz/
wall 13.3 /wɔːl/
want: Do you want me to ... 17.2
　/du ju 'wʌnt mi tuː/
warehouse 4.3 /'weəhaʊs/
warn 20 A /wɔːn/
warranty 13.1 /'wɒrənti/
waste disposal 10 C /'weɪst dɪspəʊzl/
watch (n) 7.3 /wɒtʃ/
watch (v) 7.3 /wɒtʃ/
watch: Watch out 16.1 /wɒtʃ 'aʊt/
weather 9.1 /'weðə/
week 6.2 /wiːk/
weekend 1.3 /wiː'kend/
weekly 7.2 /'wiːkli/
weight 12.2 /weɪt/
welcome 6.1 /'welkəm/
welcome: You're welcome 4.1
　/jɔː 'welkəm/
What about ... 8.2 /wɒt ə'baʊt/
What do you do? 2.1 /wɒt də ju 'duː/
white 12.2 /waɪt/
wholesaler 16.3 /'həʊseɪlə/
why don't you ... 7.3 /waɪ 'dəʊnt juː/
wide 13.2 /waɪd/
wife 14.1 /waɪf/
winter 19.1 /'wɪntə/
within 12.3 /wɪ'ðɪn/
wonder: I wonder if you could help
　me 11.1
　/aɪ wʌndə ɪf ju kʊd 'help miː/
work 1.3 /wɜːk/
work: I work in ... 2.1 /aɪ wɜːk ɪn/
work: Who do you work for? 3.1
　/hu də ju 'wɜːk fɔː/
workforce 2.1 /'wɜːkfɔːs/
working: working hours 19.2
　/'wɜːkɪŋ aʊəz/
worldwide 3.1 /wɜːld'waɪd/
worry 7.2 /'wʌri/
worry: Don't worry 17.2
　/dəʊnt 'wʌri/
worst 13.2 /wɜːst/
worth 13.1 /wɜːθ/
Would you ... 7.1 /'wʊd juː/
write 6.2 /raɪt/

year 6.2 /jɪə/
yellow 12.2 /'jeləʊ/
yet 16.2 /jet/